# DigitalFocus

## the NEW MEDIA of PHOTOGRAPHY

edited by

# KATHLEEN ZIEGLER
## and
# NICK GRECO

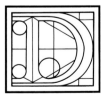

**Dimensional Illustrators, Inc.**
**Southampton, Pennsylvania USA**

**HBI**
**Hearst Books International**
**New York, NY USA**

*First Published by*
**Dimensional Illustrators, Inc.**
For Hearst Books International
1350 Avenue of the Americas
New York, NY 10019 USA

*Distributed in the USA and Canada by*
**North Light Books,**
**an imprint of F&W Publications**
1507 Dana Avenue
Cincinnati, OH 45207 USA
ISBN 0-688-15418-2

*Distributed throughout the rest of the world by*
**Hearst Books International**
1350 Avenue of the Americas
New York, NY 10019 USA
Fax: 212-261-6795
ISBN 0-688-15418-2

*First Published in Germany by*
**NIPPAN**
Nippon Shuppan Hanbai
Deutschland GmbH
Krefelder Str. 85
D-40549 Dusseldorf, Germany
0211-5048089 Telephone
0211-5049326 Fax
ISBN 3-910052-96-7

*Address Direct Mail Sales to*
**Dimensional Illustrators, Inc.**
362 2nd Street Pike/Suite 112
Southampton, PA 18966 USA
215-953-1415 *Phone*
215-953-1697 *Fax*
dimension@3DimIllus.com *Email*
http://www.3DimIllus.com *Website*

**DigitalFocus: the New Media of Photography**
Kathleen Ziegler, Nick Greco

*Printed in Singapore*

## DIGITALFOCUS CREDITS

CREATIVE DIRECTOR/ASSOCIATE EDITOR
**Kathleen Ziegler**
**Dimensional Illustrators, Inc.**

EXECUTIVE EDITOR
**Nick Greco**
**Dimensional Illustrators, Inc.**

INTERIOR DESIGN, COVER DESIGN
& TYPOGRAPHY
**Melissa Walter**
**MWdesign/Bensalem, PA**
**215-639-4181**

COPYWRITER
**Rachael Allendar**

COPY CONSULTANT
**Leona Mangol**

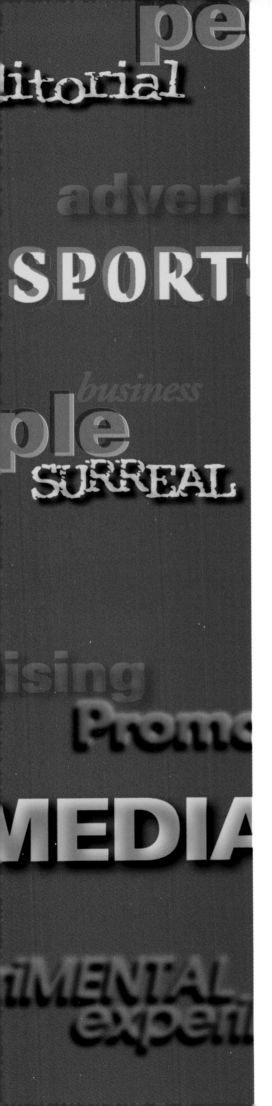

# Contents

# introduction

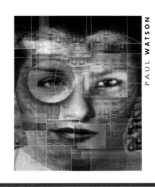

# DigitalFocus

## the NEW MEDIA of PHOTOGRAPHY

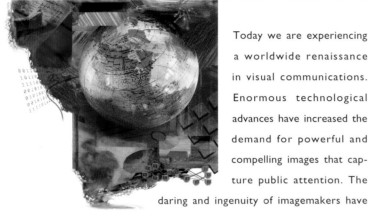

Today we are experiencing a worldwide renaissance in visual communications. Enormous technological advances have increased the demand for powerful and compelling images that capture public attention. The daring and ingenuity of imagemakers have transformed forever our understanding of the camera and the computer. The barrier that once divided photographers and digital illustrators has vanished. A door has opened on a dynamic visual universe that offers, those eager to meet the challenge, the potential and vitality of infinite design capabilities. *DigitalFocus* explores the essence of this burgeoning medium. Both explosive and impressive, the fusion of photography and digital illustration has produced a range of work that exceeds the very limits of expectation. With more than 300 full-color examples, *DigitalFocus* brings this incredible array into perspective. This premiere edition applauds the diversity of imagination and provides a detailed examination of how digital and photographic creators have combined their talents to create a new photographic genre. This powerful, new imagery transforms reality and illusion into an ever shifting metamorphic vision.

In this period of renaissance, the reciprocal exchange of conceptual and methodical acumen has afforded artists unrestrained creative license to move between the camera, the found image and the computer. Forty energetic, photo-digital professionals were invited to submit their best and most cutting-edge work. What most distinguishes this body of work is the profound differences in each of the design solutions and technical strategies. They range from painterly and surrealistic to high tech and starkly focused. Some artists rely on the cyber-palette to take the viewer on an interactive journey through cyberspace and others subtly enhance minute details. Creative techniques and software choices are also highly varied. Some photos are generated in-camera using a single application while others incorporate the manipulation and design fabrication of various programs. Each artist has developed a personal, distinct style that encompasses a spontaneous method of collage and layering, to carefully planned formats that expose a complex spatial language. To highlight the diverse nature of the industry, forty featured images take us from concept to execution. The underlying critical thinking is discussed and the software and techniques used to create the final composition are unraveled. They demonstrate the interrelationships that exist between the origin of the idea, the creative process, and the final image.

*DigitalFocus* presents a vibrant gallery of imagery that fully showcases the scope of work being produced that aptly demonstrates the intense influence of electronic photography on all aspects of visual communi-

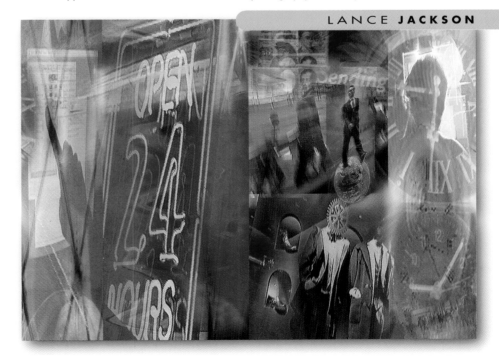

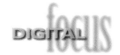

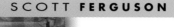

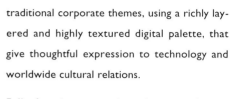

cations. Presented in nine sections, the work represents the genre of professional photo-digital images embedded with emotional expression and visual approach. The chapters -- Advertising, Business, Sports, People, Media, Editorial, Surreal, Promotional, and Experimental — expose these daring new visionaries who allow experimentation and experience to create a dynamic, visual landscape that impacts every facet of the commercial communication industry.

In the *advertising* chapter, the attention of the viewer is captured by a digital melange of provocative photos, powerful software effects and an intoxicating palette of invigorating images. Convincing advertisements, campaigns, brochures and posters are strengthened by the symbolic connotations that evoke a compelling visual language. Intimating and bold, energetic and striking, they provoke an unforgettable visual impact.

The world of *business* demands its own carefully orchestrated approach. The fast-paced, high-tech global community mandates images that reflect trends within the communication arena. Sophisticated and effectively meaningful strategies are presented with

traditional corporate themes, using a richly layered and highly textured digital palette, that give thoughtful expression to technology and worldwide cultural relations.

Full of excitement and motion, *sport* images carry the intensity of speed and the drama of competition. Exaggerated and imposing, unconstrained photographic perspective is combined with the fine-tuning capabilities of the computer to attain images that fully convey the graceful gestures and powerful attitude present in athletics. Sweeping figures of intense spirit reveal the profound impact of sports today.

Personal identities are exposed in the *people* chapter. Character emotions are portrayed through the integration of the face as a central, visual and conceptual component. Compound layering, collage and juxtaposition of elements reflect the multifaceted aspects of each individual. This eerie blending of visuals reveals layers of metaphoric meaning and encode complex messages into simple facial features.

Exploring the very boundaries of time and space, *media* looks at the most current and adventuresome design projects being developed today. Suspended in time on the printed page, the websites, CD Roms,

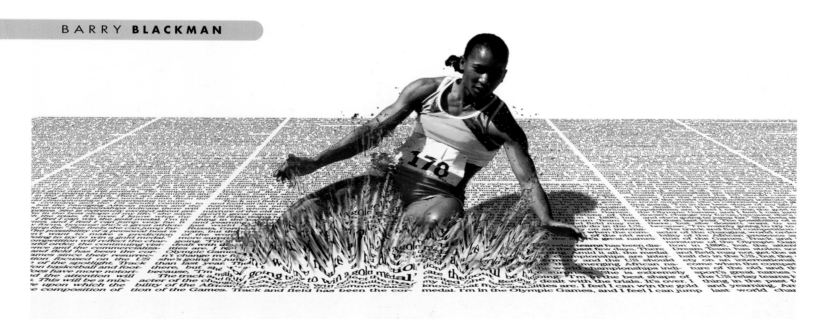

*duction* *introduction* introduction

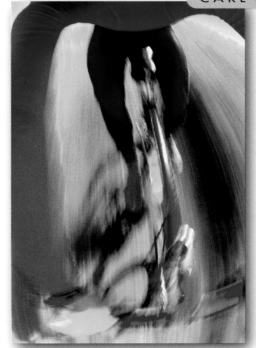

CARL **SCHNEIDER**

and software visuals float through the illusionary perception of space.

With the goal of accurately illustrating and illuminating, the *editorial* section gives emotional impact to the message of the adjoining text. The key is clearly defining the essential meaning and finding a visual language to implement it precise expression. Uncompromising and direct, the images link meaning and emphasize critical issues. The reader is presented with compelling visuals that embellish the editorial.

The blend of mesmerizing photography and digital drama is uncovered in the *surreal* chapter. Illusionary compositions haunt the viewer as hidden metaphoric symbols unfold. Articulate and deeply layered, obscure messages draw the viewer into a complex and subliminally unsettling world. In the surreal environment, the spectator is held captive by its hypnotic effect.

The *promotional* chapter offers the opportunity to establish a creative identity. This self representation displays both conceptual strength and a distinctive visual style. Versatile and exuberant, the images express technical capabilities while promoting confidence and a wider clientele base.

Entirely free of restraints, the *experimental* chapter offers the daring individual a dynamic set of unlimited creative tools. The inner voice finds expression as the mind and intuition are given space to explore. Personal and effective, the work reflects an extensive visual range that transform, internal visions into perceptive images.

Once a novelty, the computer is the visual illustrator's most essential creative vehicle. As we near a new millennium, the digital revolution has soared beyond all expectations. No one could have predicted the innovative and dramatic possibilities that have emerged through the fusion of photography and digital imagery. Each new technological advance has given rise to another exciting shift and a new burst of dynamic exploration. In this constantly evolving field, we offer *DigitalFocus* as a celebration of the bold vision of photographers and illustrators as they influence the future.

—*Kathleen Ziegler and Nick Greco*

# ADVERTISING
*advertising*

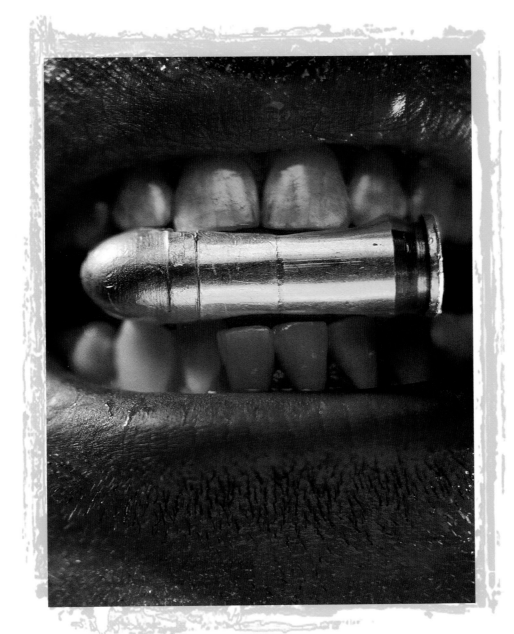

# NICK KOUDIS

**AUSTRALIAN FOR ANESTHETIC**

*PHOTOGRAPHER*
**Nick Koudis**

*DIGITAL CREATIVE*
**Nick Koudis**

*CLIENT*
**Fosters Lager**

*SOFTWARE*
**Adobe Photoshop**

*CATEGORY*
**Advertisement**

No subject remains ordinary when approached by Nick Koudis. This bold, arresting image was produced for an ad campaign for Fosters beer. It appeared on billboards and in print and was used as a self-promotional. Vivid and confrontational, the work relies on taut photographic qualities for its piercing visual impact and digital effects to further enhance the charged mood.

The image of the teeth biting the bullet was made in-camera and then scanned into Adobe Photoshop. The use of an extreme close-up and the tightly clenched jaw creates an underlying sense of tension. Digitally amplified color contrast and saturation heighten the focus on the bullet and gives the final photograph dynamic energy.

Blending his sharp wit with a daring vision, Koudis finds inventive and invigorating design solutions for all his projects. He integrates traditional photography and digital possibilities by concentrating on details and nuance. This subtle approach creates broad and compelling undercurrents of meaning and produces impressively memorable results.

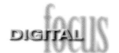

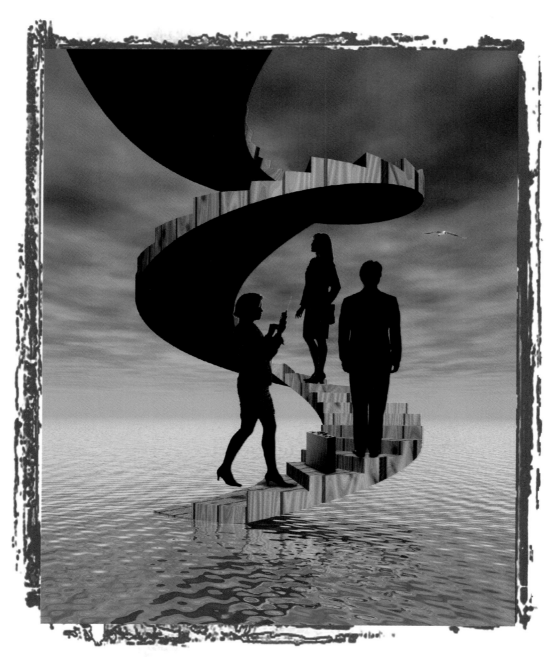

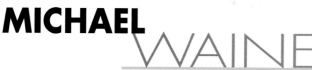

# MICHAEL WAINE

**EXECUTIVES RISING**

The corporate climb to success is cleverly presented in this illustration by Michael Waine. Rising out of the ocean, the winding staircase leads slowly upward to a hidden goal. By placing the executives near the base of the steps, it becomes clear that the ascent will not be easy. Produced as a conceptual image, this piece was created for a stock photo agency in New York known as The Stock Market.

The background, sky and stairs were rendered in KPT Bryce. These components, along with the photographic elements of the figures, were brought into Adobe Photoshop and assembled. Adjustments were implemented to the colors and shadows.

In "Executives Rising" Waine dynamically captures the essential meaning behind a familiar concept. His intriguing background helps to abstract and focus the image, while the choice of a spiral staircase emphasizes the challenge of reaching the top. His unique approach gives this illustration a refreshing originality.

*PHOTOGRAPHER*
**Michael Waine**

*DIGITAL CREATIVE*
**Michael Waine**

*CLIENT*
**Conceptual Stock Image**

*SOFTWARE*
**Adobe Photoshop**

*CATEGORY*
**Advertising**

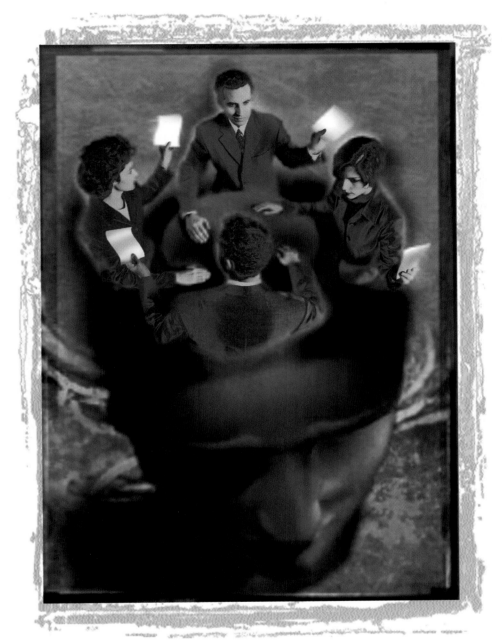

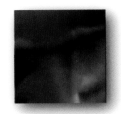

**MAKE IT YOUR BUSINESS**

*PHOTOGRAPHER*
**Daniel Arsenault**

*DIGITAL CREATIVE*
**Rob Magiera**

*CLIENT*
**First Security Bank**

*SOFTWARE*
**Adobe Photoshop,
Alias Power Animator**

*CATEGORY*
**Institutional / In-House
Promotional Campaign**

# MAGIERA ROB

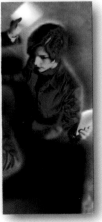

Created by Rob Magiera of Noumena for an in-house campaign to promote a new business expansion program for First Security Bank, this image expressively illustrates thought in action. The original concept was developed by The Hurst Group ad agency. Magiera then worked with the art director to envision a harmonious design that would be possible to create. The idea was to depict a bank client's head, superimposed with the bank divisions, working as a team.

Digital mannequins were used to establish the body positions and general layout. The four live models were posed and photographed based on this initial digital template. The 3D-statue head was generated in Alias Power Animator. The subtle textured background image was produced by scanning a sheet of rusted metal. All the elements were imported into Adobe Photoshop. Layers were created and the composition was adjusted and repositioned to form an overall balance. A rich color palette was selected and manipulated to suggest an expansive sense of illumination.

For more than ten years, Magiera has been producing elegant and engaging visual solutions for print, video and computer projects. His thoughtful response to creative challenges is even captured in the name of his studio, Noumena, a derivative of the Greek word for "think."

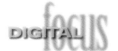

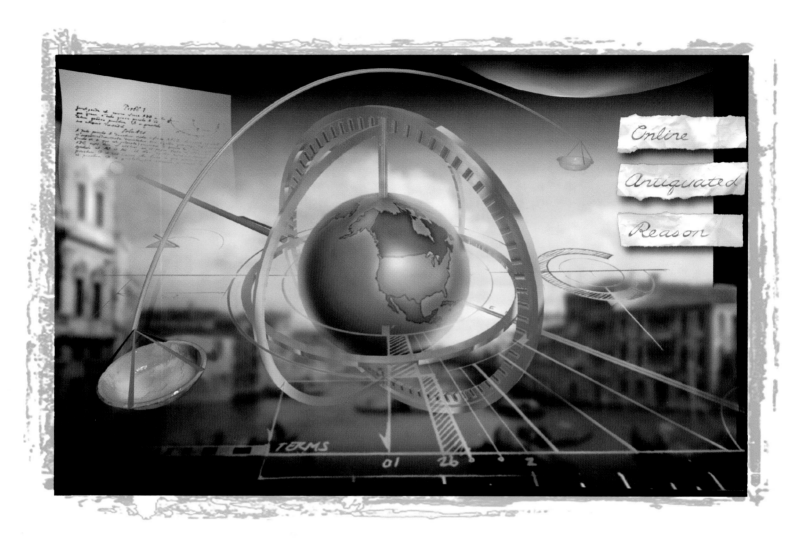

# HENK DAWSON

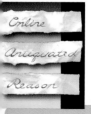

## ANTIQUATED REASON

**Created** to promote a conference on copyright issues, this image gracefully blends distinct visual elements as it explores a highly intellectual issue. Through symbolic language, the concern for balancing fairness and justice, where laws and attitudes are varied, is represented. In his choice of background, Henk Dawson suggests a history of Old World tradition. The long arc of the scale begins in the softly focused past, extends across the globe and tips into sharp present day contrast. This implies the far reaching, modern complexity that must be weighed in the question of copyright.

**Dawson** first creates a pencil sketch to determine the feasibility of his concept. Foreground elements were rendered using Form Z. The lighting and textures were added in Electric Image. Finally, Adobe Photoshop was used to assemble the completed image and modify the luminance, color and softness.

**An** unsaturated color palette and soft focus are signatures of Dawson's compositions. More than ten years of experience enables him to transform esoteric concepts into relevant, appealing illustration.

**PHOTOGRAPHER**
Henk Dawson/Stock

**DIGITAL CREATIVE**
Henk Dawson

**CLIENT**
Graphic Artists Guild,
Hewlett Packard

**SOFTWARE**
Form Z, Electric Image,
Adobe Photoshop

**CATEGORY**
Advertising

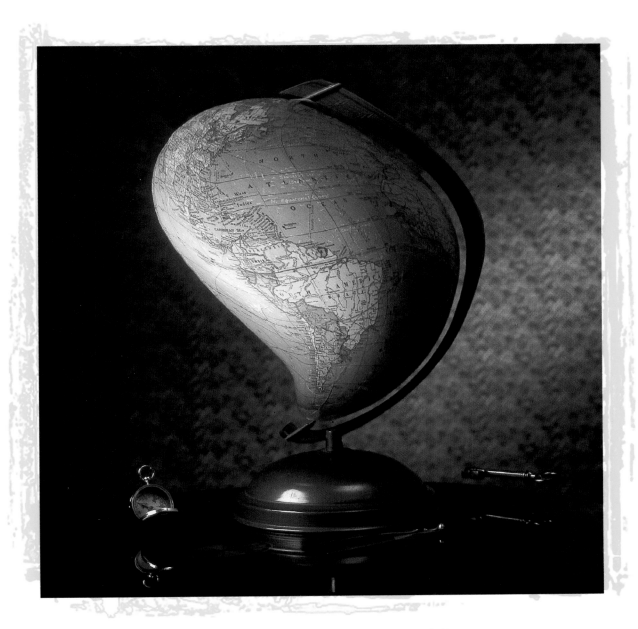

## J.W. BURKEY

**WARPED GLOBE**

*PHOTOGRAPHER*
**J.W. Burkey**

*DIGITAL CREATIVE*
**J.W. Burkey**

*ART DIRECTOR*
**Jonathan Rice**

*CLIENT*
**Blanks Color Imaging**

*SOFTWARE*
**Metaflow, Adobe Photoshop**

*CATEGORY*
**Advertising**

**J. W. Burkey** was asked to create a photograph for DDB Needham's client, Blanks Color Imaging, showing the capabilities of their digital camera. His playfully surreal design solution fully utilizes the unique qualities of the product.

**To** demonstrate the magical tricks of levitation and object bending, Burkey relied on the camera's ability to shoot a series of exposures in perfect registration. He then repositioned and photographed the props to produce the overall image. The shape of the globe was altered using Metaflo. The final assemblage, masking and color corrections were done in Adobe Photoshop.

**This** filmless photographic image highlights the most recent advances in digital technology. Burkey's twelve years of experience have enabled him to balance humor and mystery. From comic to cosmic, his creative vision is on the cutting-edge.

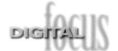

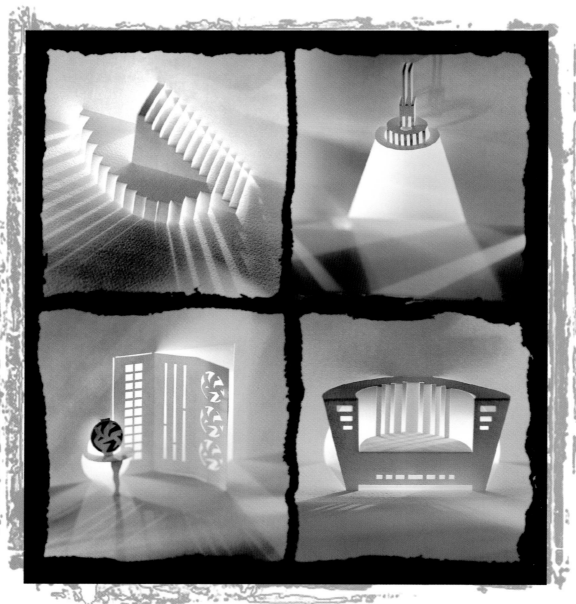

# BILL MILNE

**The** unique, expressive mood captured in these four panels by Bill Milne poetically carries the viewer into a magical world. These images appeared in advertisements, posters and promotional materials for the International Furniture Fair held in New York. Deceptively simple, this work balances the delicate and the dramatic through use of subtle dimensionality and theatrical lighting.

**Original** paper sculpture transparencies were scanned into Adobe Photoshop. The application of filters diffused the highlights and deepened the shadows creating the painterly patterns. Alterations were applied to the borders of each image to reinforce the qualities captured in the lighting. Four color separations were generated to produce fine tones, while retaining a sense of black and white.

**Milne's** work ranges from vibrant high-tech to the wonderfully understated image. In this impressive example, he stages a playful drama through his thoughtful use of restraint. Milne is comfortable with his ability to provide distinctive design solutions that integrate the natural world and the magic of technology.

## VARIATIONS OF FURNITURE

*PHOTOGRAPHER*
**Bill Milne**

*DIGITAL CREATIVE*
**Bill Milne**

*CLIENT*
**International Furniture Fair**

*SOFTWARE*
**Adobe Photoshop**

*CATEGORY*
**Advertising**

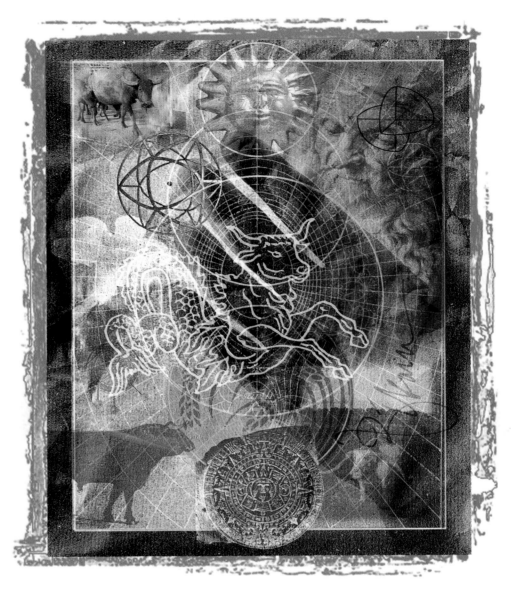

# JOSEPH KELTER

**This** image was originally created as an illustration for a calendar. The work focuses on Bikara, an ox who is the Guardian God of February. In this multi-layered collage, mystical symbols and delicately embedded text are blended with rich colors to suggest the relationship between Bikara and nature.

**Joseph Kelter** began this project by researching the images on the Internet. An initial pencil sketch was scanned into Macromedia Freehand to create the overall proportions and shape of the finished design. The Freehand file was then imported into Macromedia XRes and the masking, textures and intricate layering were added. Images selected from original photographs and stock art were assembled and revised until the proportions were correct. The feeling of depth was accomplished by varying opacity and compositing modes. Final adjustments and color corrections were completed in Adobe Photoshop.

**A** fine arts artist with a degree in painting and illustration, Kelter has used the electronic media since the early 80s. His flexible design approach allows him to create images where technology is submerged and concepts emerge.

**BIKARA**

*PHOTOGRAPHER*
**Joseph Kelter, Various Stock Images**

*DIGITAL CREATIVE*
**BadCat Design, Inc.**

*CLIENT*
**Matsuzaki Ink, WACE**

*SOFTWARE*
**Macromedia xRes, Adobe Photoshop**

*CATEGORY*
**Advertising**

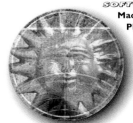

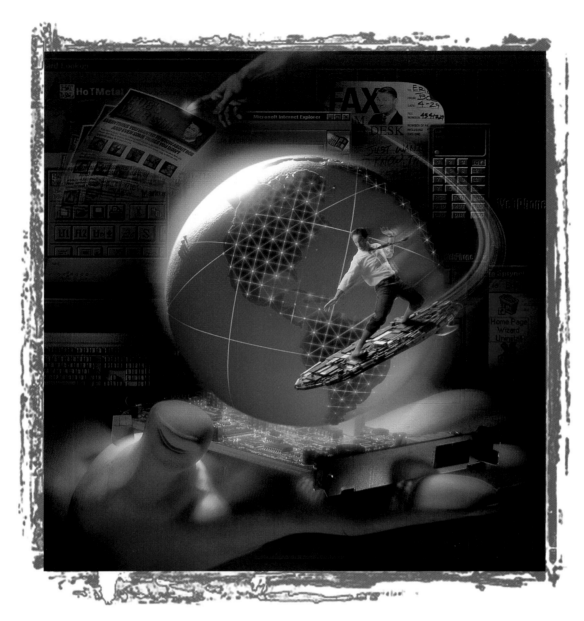

# RICHARD
## WAHLSTROM

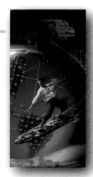

**WORLD SURFER**

*PHOTOGRAPHER*
**Richard Wahlstrom**

*DIGITAL CREATIVE*
**Richard Wahlstrom**

*CLIENT*
**Creative Labs**

*SOFTWARE*
**Adobe Photoshop**

*CATEGORY*
**Advertising**

**Richard Wahlstrom's** illustration, advertising the capabilities of Creative Labs' communications card for World Wide Web surfing, depicts a balance between security and fun. The professional, pants rolled up and tie flying, leans back to enjoy a fast-paced global ride, firmly supported by a surfboard made of computer components. The serene strength of the supportive hand balances the surfer, and indicates the safe environment in which such a ride takes place.

**Initially**, numerous photographic elements were scanned into Adobe Photoshop. Background imagery was layered into a collage and softened with filters. The foreground items were highlighted and a blur effect was added to convey motion. A broad color palette was selected to distinguish various aspects and enhance the mood of this playful photograph.

**The** background elements give a clear sense of the power and capabilities of the product. They underscore and strengthen the message of potential freedom and pleasure available, when proper equipment provides support. Richard Wahlstrom's clever approach is an engaging treatment of a multifaceted subject.

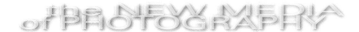

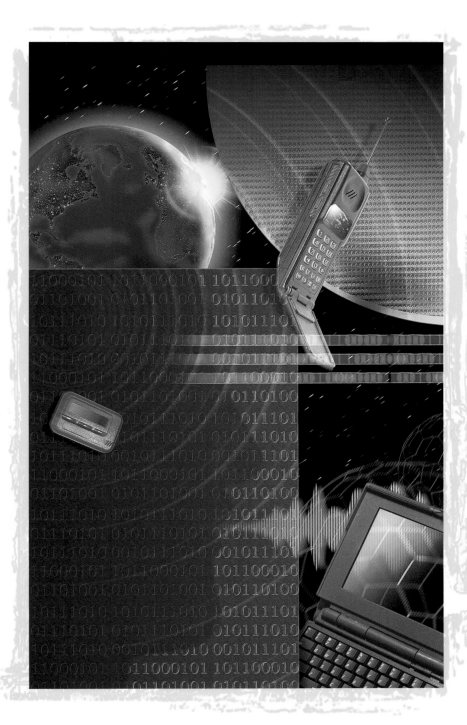

# STEVEN HUNT

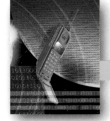

**This** crisp image presents the dynamics of modern communication, illustrating voice and data information accessibility. Through the thoughtful inclusion of essential icons, Steven Hunt explores the importance of advances in technology and the concept of global connectivity.

**Hunt** initially fabricated graphic elements in Adobe Illustrator. These, along with photographic components, were imported into Adobe Photoshop. Some of the elements were first masked, then assembled in layers. To provide striking emphasis, the vibrant color palette was designed using complementary hues and variations in saturation.

**Through** easily understood symbols, this image conveys the complex nature of message transmission. The subtle human silhouette acts to anchor the work both conceptually and formally. Radiating from the figure, words and data are projected indefinitely. Including the glowing sun and the cosmic background suggests the universal need for intercommunication. The power of Hunt's design lies in his spontaneous evolutionary approach — resulting in visually exciting imagery.

## DIGITAL COMMUNICATIONS

*PHOTOGRAPHER*
**Steven Hunt**

*DIGITAL CREATIVE*
**Steven Hunt**

*CLIENT*
**Canadian Wireless
Communications**

*SOFTWARE*
**Adobe Photoshop**

*CATEGORY*
**Advertising**

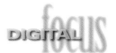

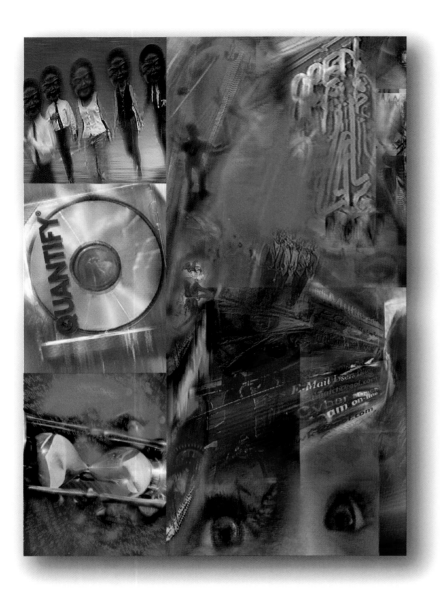

**NIMS 95**

*PHOTOGRAPHER & VIDEO*
Lance Jackson

*DIGITAL CREATIVES*
Clay James, Craig Ing, Laura Stoll

*CLIENT*
Motorola, Informix & Sunworld

*SOFTWARE*
Adobe Photoshop

*CATEGORY*
Advertising

**ALT PICK 96. MADONNA IN FLIGHT**

*PHOTOGRAPHER & VIDEO*
Lance Jackson

*DIGITAL CREATIVE*
Lance Jackson

*CLIENT*
Al Riney & Associates

*SOFTWARE*
Adobe Photoshop

*CATEGORY*
Advertising

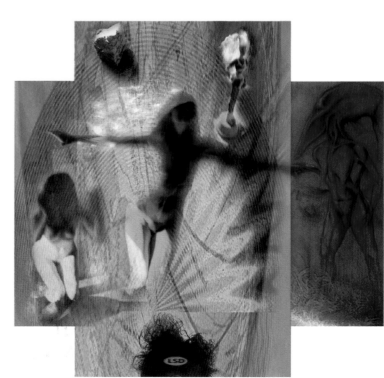

ADVERTISING *advertising*

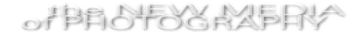

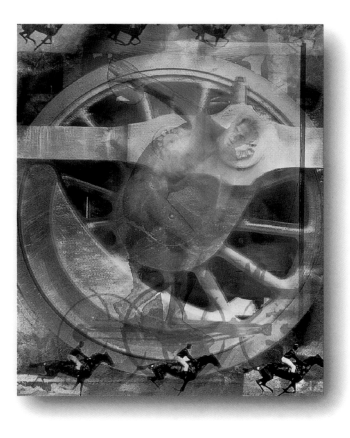

## COMPETITION

**PHOTOGRAPHER**
Scott Ferguson

**DIGITAL CREATIVE**
Scott Ferguson

**ART DIRECTOR**
Deanna Kuhlman

**CLIENT**
Mead Paper Company

**SOFTWARE**
Live Picture, Fractal Design's Painter,
Adobe Illustrator, Adobe Photoshop

**CATEGORY**
Advertising

## OPEN 24 HOURS. GEAR HEAD

**PHOTOGRAPHER & VIDEO**
Lance Jackson

**DIGITAL CREATIVE**
Christa McDonald

**CLIENT**
Compuserve

**SOFTWARE**
Adobe Photoshop

**CATEGORY**
Advertising Media Kit

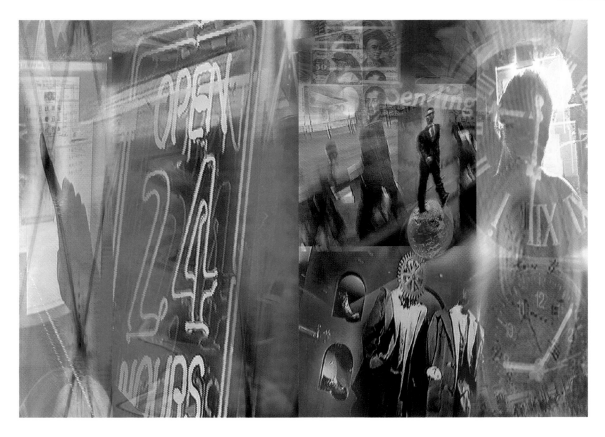

Advertising Advertising advertisi

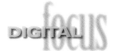

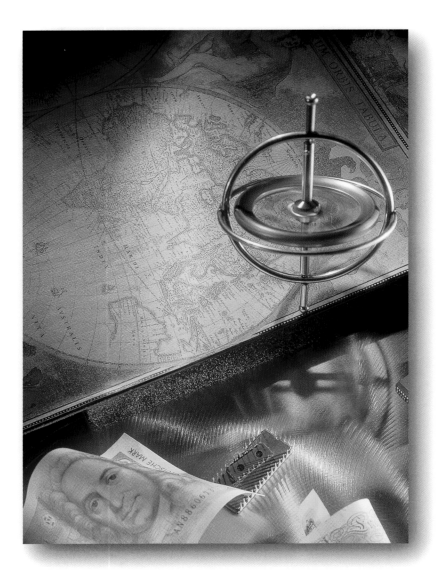

## GOLD GYROSCOPE

*PHOTOGRAPHER*
**Stan Musilek**

*DIGITAL CREATIVE*
**Stan Musilek**

*CLIENT*
**Microsoft**

*SOFTWARE*
**Live Pictures**

*CATEGORY*
**Advertising**

## POLAR EYEWEAR

*PHOTOGRAPHER*
**Bill Milne**

*DIGITAL CREATIVE*
**Bill Milne**

*CLIENT*
**Younger Optics**

*SOFTWARE*
**Adobe Photoshop,
Adobe Illustrator**

*CATEGORY*
**Advertising**

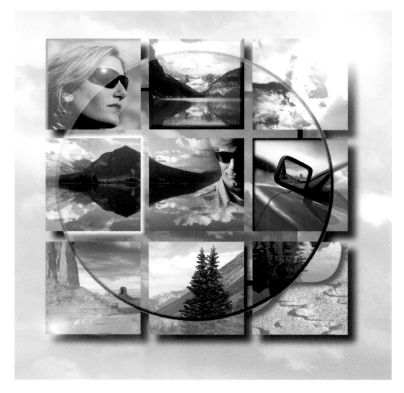

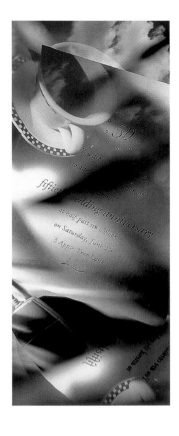
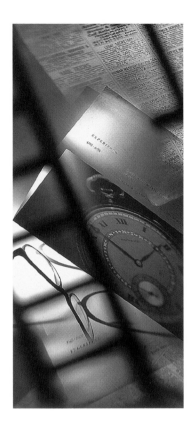
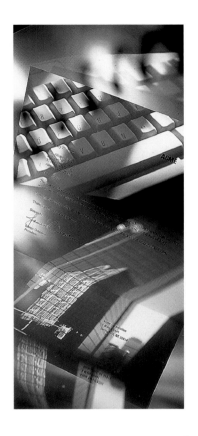

**TRIPTYCH**

*PHOTOGRAPHER*
Logan Seale

*DIGITAL CREATIVES*
Logan Seale, Ellen Hartshorne

*CLIENT*
Champion Paper

*SOFTWARE*
Adobe Photoshop

*CATEGORY*
Advertising

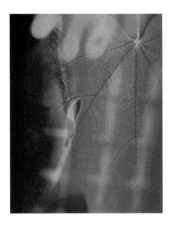
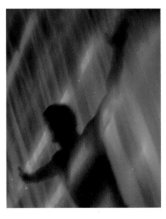
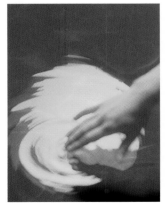
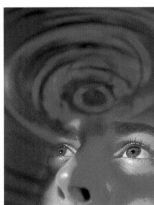

**CANON SERIES**

*PHOTOGRAPHERS*
Sharon White/Bob Packert

*DIGITAL CREATIVES*
Sharon White/Bob Packert

*CLIENT*
Canon Color Printers

*SOFTWARE*
Adobe Photoshop, Live Picture

*CATEGORY*
Advertising

Advertising Advertising *advertisi*

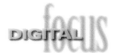

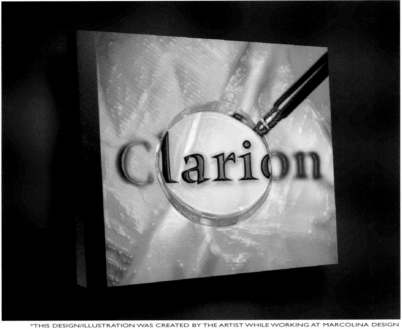

*THIS DESIGN/ILLUSTRATION WAS CREATED BY THE ARTIST WHILE WORKING AT MARCOLINA DESIGN

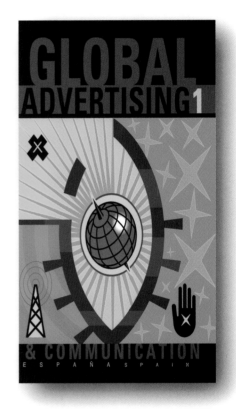

### "CLARION"

*LETRASET FONT PROMO*

*DIGITAL CREATIVE*
Matthew Peacock*
Anonymous Productions

*CLIENT*
Letraset Corporation

*SOFTWARE*
Adobe Photoshop,
Adobe Illustrator

*CATEGORY*
Advertising

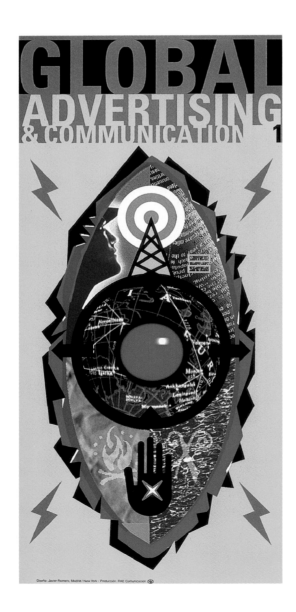

### RAE POSTER

*DIGITAL CREATIVE*
JRDG

*CLIENT*
RAE Publishing
Barcelona

*SOFTWARE*
Adobe Illustrator,
Adobe Photoshop

*CATEGORY*
Poster

### RAE COVER

*DIGITAL CREATIVE*
JRDG

*CLIENT*
RAE Publishing / Barcelona

*SOFTWARE*
Adobe Illustrator

*CATEGORY*
Book Cover

ADVERTISING *advertising*

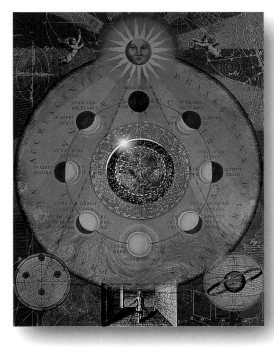

### SUN, MOON AND STARS

*PHOTOGRAPHERS*
Joseph Kelter, Planet Art Digital

*DIGITAL CREATIVE*
BadCat Design, Inc.

*CLIENT*
Planet Art

*SOFTWARE*
Specular Collage, Adobe Photoshop

*CATEGORY*
Advertising

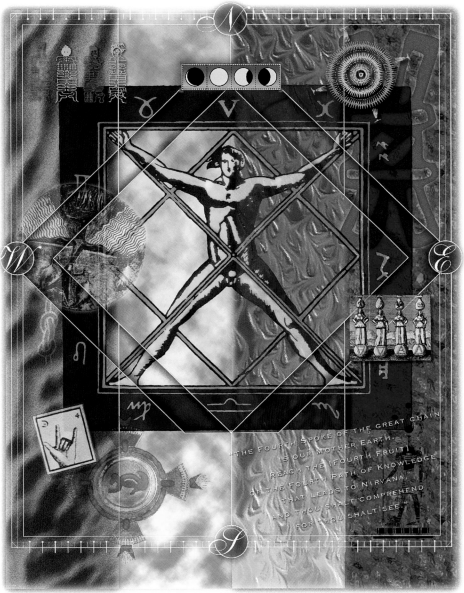

### THE MATERIAL ORDER

*PHOTOGRAPHER*
Joeseph Kelter, Various Stock Images

*DIGITAL CREATIVE*
BadCat Design, Inc.

*CLIENT*
Specular International

*SOFTWARE*
Specular Collage, Adobe Photoshop,
Fractal Design's Painter

*CATEGORY*
Advertising

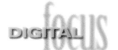

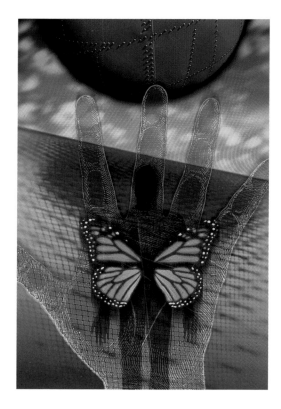

## ABSOLUT LOGO

**DIGITAL CREATIVE**
JRDG

**CLIENT**
Advertising Age Magazine

**SOFTWARE**
Ray Dream Designer, Alias

**CATEGORY**
Advertising

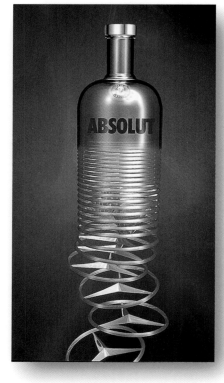

### METAMORPHOSIS OF SOUL

**PHOTOGRAPHER**
Steven Hunt

**DIGITAL CREATIVE**
Steven Hunt

**CLIENT**
Nick Johnson Productions

**SOFTWARE**
Adobe Photoshop

**CATEGORY**
Advertising

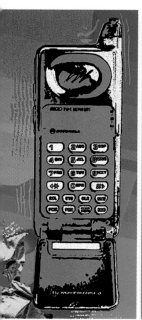
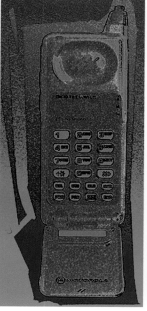
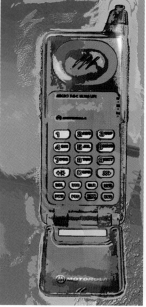
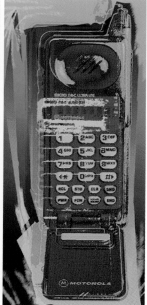

### BILLBOARDS

**DIGITAL CREATIVE**
Philip Howe

**ART DIRECTOR**
Paul Matthaeus

**CLIENT**
GTE

**SOFTWARE**
Adobe Photoshop, Fractal Design's Painter

**CATEGORY**
Billboard Advertising

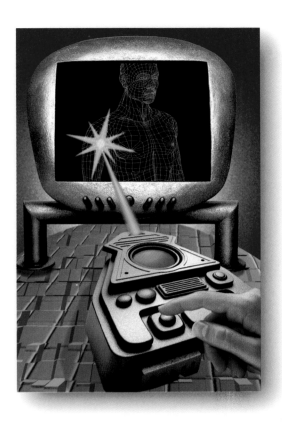

## LORTAB MONITOR

*PHOTOGRAPHER*
Michael Waine

*DIGITAL CREATIVE*
Michael Waine

*CLIENT*
UCB Pharma, Inc.

*SOFTWARE*
Adobe Photoshop

*CATEGORY*
Advertising

## THE NET

*PHOTOGRAPHER*
Michael Waine

*DIGITAL CREATIVE*
Michael Waine

*CLIENT*
Stock Conceptual Image

*SOFTWARE*
Adobe Photoshop

*CATEGORY*
Advertising

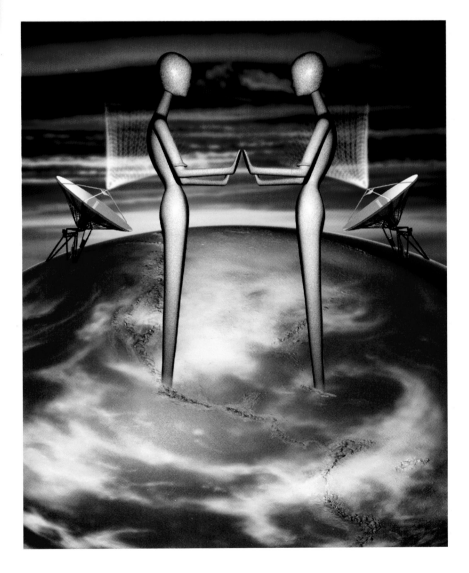

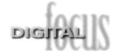

**REFLECTIONS OF NAPA VALLEY**

*PHOTOGRAPHER*
**Richard Walstrom**

*DIGITAL CREATIVE*
**Richard Walstrom**

*CLIENT*
**Napa Valley Vinters Association**

*SOFTWARE*
**Adobe Photoshop**

*CATEGORY*
**Advertising**

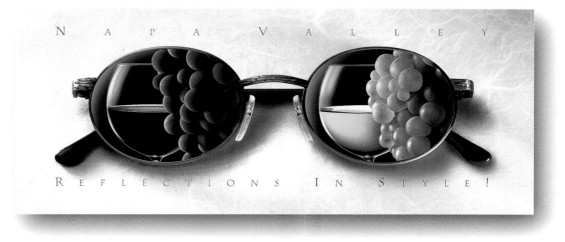

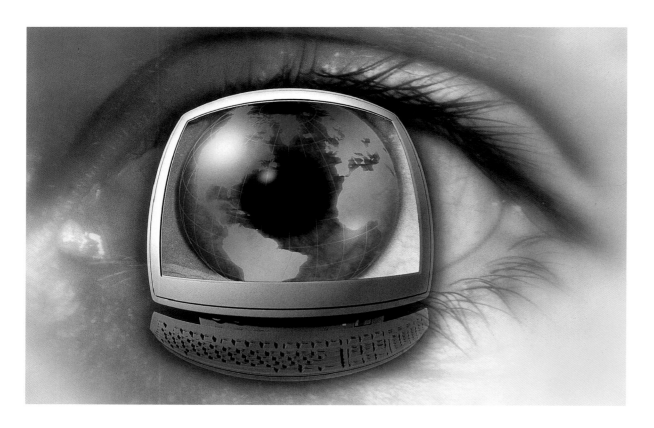

**THE EYES OF THE INTERNET**

*PHOTOGRAPHER*
**Steven Hunt**

*DIGITAL CREATIVE*
**Steven Hunt**

*CLIENT*
**Motorola Corporation**

*SOFTWARE*
**Adobe Photoshop**

*CATEGORY*
**Advertising**

ADVERTISING *advertising*

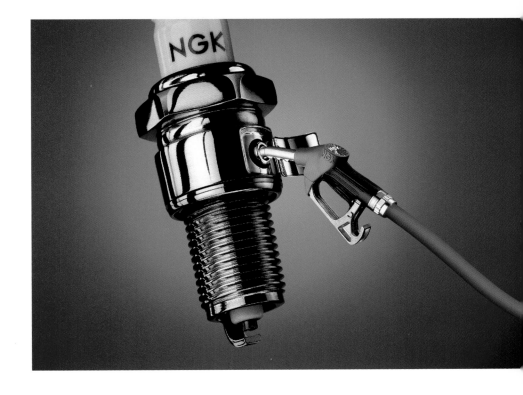

### SPARK PLUG

*PHOTOGRAPHER*
Rick Dunn

*DIGITAL CREATIVE*
Rick Dunn

*CLIENT*
NGK U.K.

*SOFTWARE*
Adobe Photoshop

*CATEGORY*
Advertising

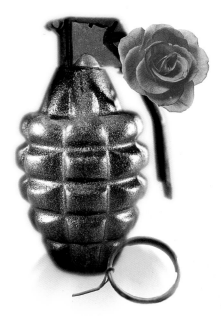

### GRENADE/ROSE

*PHOTOGRAPHER*
Michael Waine

*DIGITAL CREATIVE*
Michael Waine

*CLIENT*
Conceptual Stock Image

*SOFTWARE*
Adobe Photoshop

*CATEGORY*
Advertising

### WATCH

*PHOTOGRAPHER*
J.W. Burkey

*DIGITAL CREATIVE*
J.W. Burkey

*CLIENT*
Spectradyne, RBMM Design

*SOFTWARE*
Fractal Design's Painter,
Adobe Photoshop

*CATEGORY*
Advertising

*ART DIRECTORS*
Janet Cowling,
D.C. Stipp

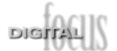

## FLOODED OFFICE

*PHOTOGRAPHER*
**Richard Wahlstrom**

*DIGITAL CREATIVE*
**Richard Wahlstrom**

*CLIENT*
**Bell South**

*SOFTWARE*
**Adobe Photoshop**

*CATEGORY*
**Advertising**

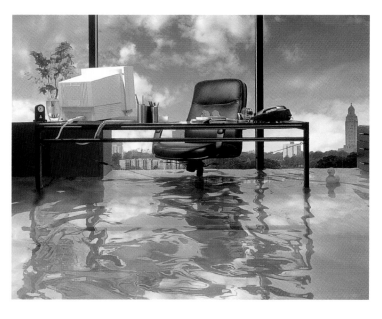

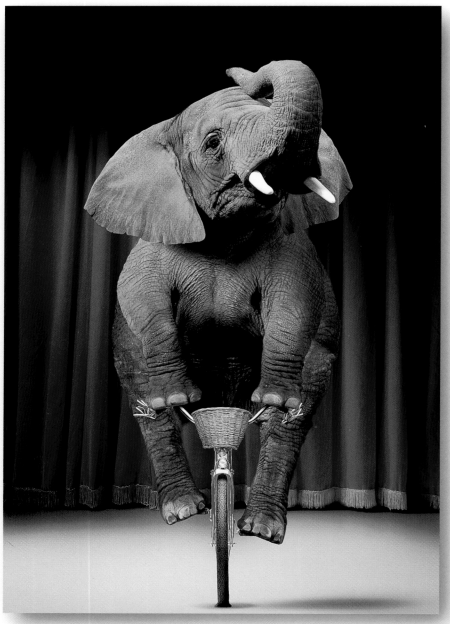

## ELEPHANT ON BIKE

*PHOTOGRAPHER*
**Richard Wahlstrom**

*DIGITAL CREATIVE*
**Richard Wahlstrom**

*CLIENT*
**Hewlett Packard**

*SOFTWARE*
**Adobe Photoshop**

*CATEGORY*
**Advertising**

ADVERTISING *advertising*

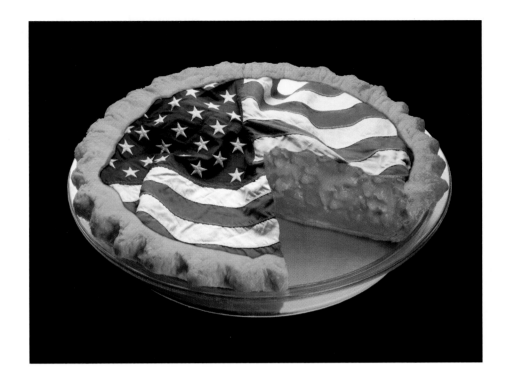

## AMERICAN PIE

**PHOTOGRAPHER**
Michael Waine

**DIGITAL CREATIVE**
Michael Waine

**CLIENT**
Conceptual Stock Image

**SOFTWARE**
Adobe Photoshop

**CATEGORY**
Advertising

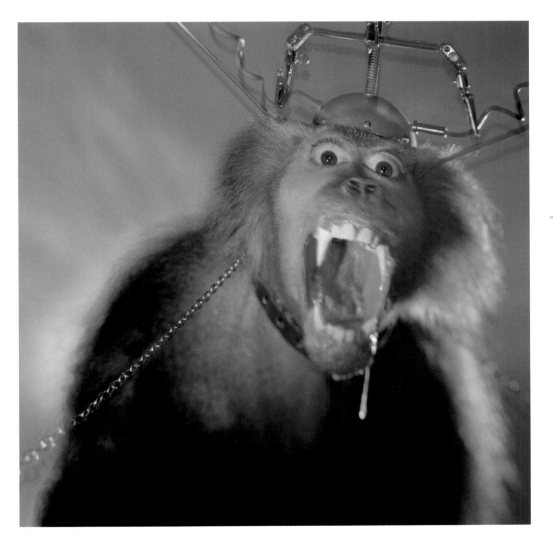

## MONKEY

**PHOTOGRAPHER**
Nick Koudis

**DIGITAL CREATIVE**
Koudis Nick

**CLIENT**
Comedy Central

**SOFTWARE**
Adobe Photoshop

**CATEGORY**
Advertising

sports

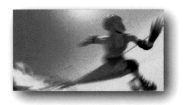

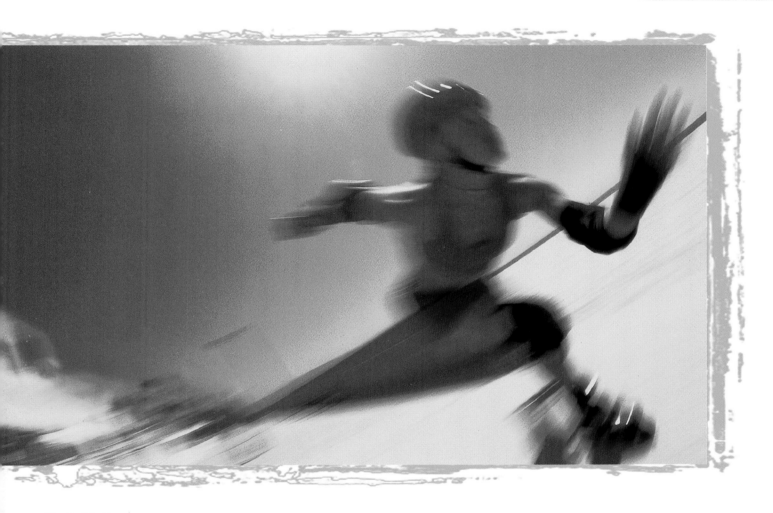

# CARL SCHNEIDER

The fast-paced world of athletic prowess is dynamically captured in this advertisement, by sports photographer, Carl Schneider. Disturbingly large and exaggeratively imposing, the skater looms past in split-second time. He wanted to portray the individuality and freedom of women athletes from an unconstrained perspective.

Using a 16mm fish-eye lens, he positioned himself within a marginal proximity of the figure. This extreme angle permitted him to distort the shape and surrounding background because he was literally feet from the subject. Shooting with a slow shutter speed, he panned the action, resulting in an intense sense of motion. Once the photo was scanned into Adobe Photoshop, it was converted from RGB to greyscale, then duotone. Next he applied his quadtone secret formula and fine-tuned the curves and tones. Selected areas were masked and final adjustments were implemented.

Schneider's photographs chronicle the extreme pace of today's athletics. His figures reveal a fresh efficiency while attaining a powerful attitude. An intense energy is coupled with graceful gestures of tireless spirit. The viewer, no longer a spectator, is captured in the suspended motion of the action.

PHOTOGRAPHER
Carl Schneider

DIGITAL CREATIVE
Carl Schneider

CLIENT
Kaiser Permanente

SOFTWARE
Adobe Photoshop

CATEGORY
Advertising

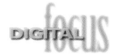

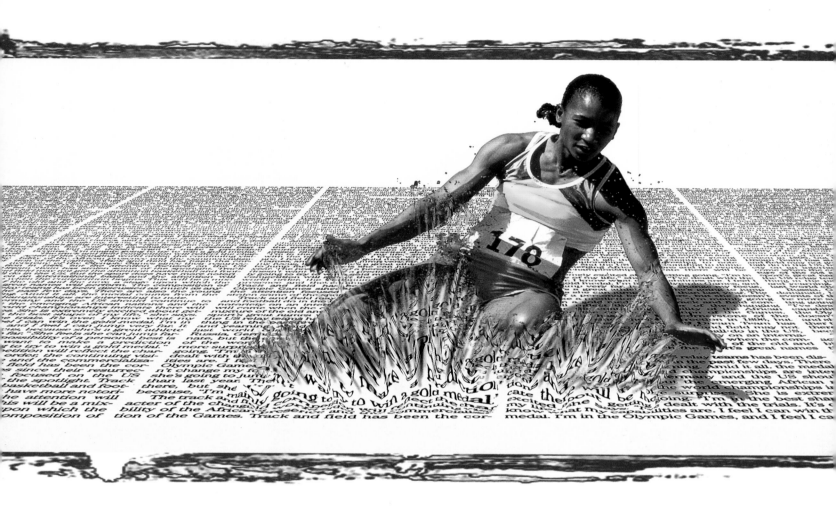

# BARRY BLACKMAN

NOBODY BRINGS YOU THE OLYMPIC GAMES LIKE THE BOSTON GLOBE

**Faced** with the challenge of photographically illustrating a series of advertisements to highlight The Boston Globe's coverage of the Olympiad, Barry Blackman created these exhilarating and dynamic images. The link between the plane of the newspaper page and the excitement of the action is gracefully captured in a visual strategy that allows words and athletes to interact. The readable text extends and heightens the visual message by placing it within the competitiveness of the Olympic Games.

**The** photographs of the athletes and newspaper were first imported into Barco Creator. Visual depth of the paper pages was achieved by altering the perspective. The waves, splashes, creases, wrinkles, and tears were then applied to the surface. Figures and text were merged together with bold shadows and a selective use of color added to the potent drama of the images.

*PHOTOGRAPHER*
**Barry Blackman, Stock**

*DIGITAL CREATIVE*
**Barry Blackman**

*CLIENT*
**Boston Globe**

*SOFTWARE*
**Barco Creator**

*CATEGORY*
**Advertising**

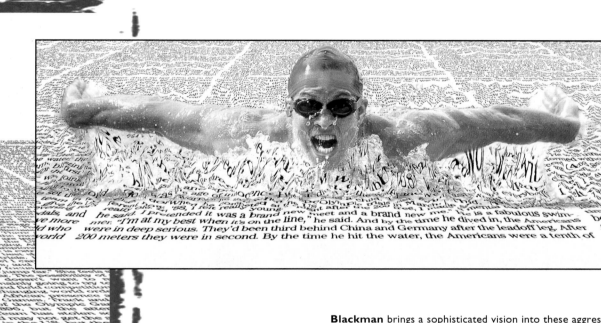

**Blackman** brings a sophisticated vision into these aggressive and captivating images by forming a bridge between the motion and energy of the sport and the ability of language to capture it. This successful series appeared both in print and on billboards, and shows the diversity and flexibility of an effectively rendered concept. Blackman's years of experience have lead to a powerful body of work which was recently published by Van Nostrand Reinhold in a book entitled, *Creating Digital Illusions / The Barry Blackman Portfolio.*

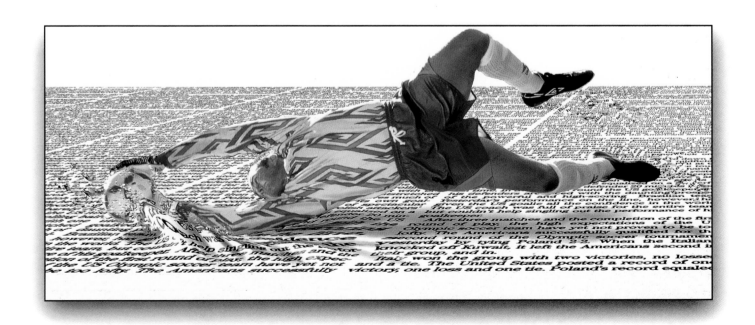

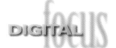

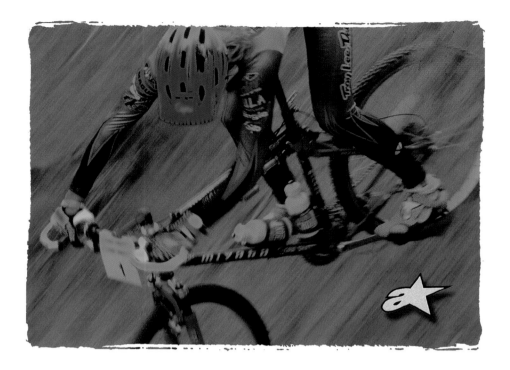

**HERBOLD**

*PHOTOGRAPHER*
Marcelo Coelho

*DIGITAL CREATIVE*
Caesar Lima

*CLIENT*
Alpinestars, Italy

*SOFTWARE*
Adobe Photoshop

*CATEGORY*
Advertising

**MOTOX**

*PHOTOGRAPHER*
Caesar Lima

*DIGITAL CREATIVE*
Caesar Lima

*CLIENT*
ONeal USA

*SOFTWARE*
Adobe Photoshop

*CATEGORY*
Advertising

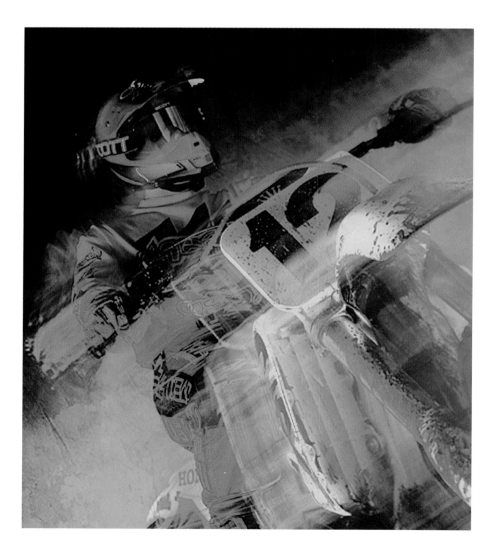

## GATORADE BREAK

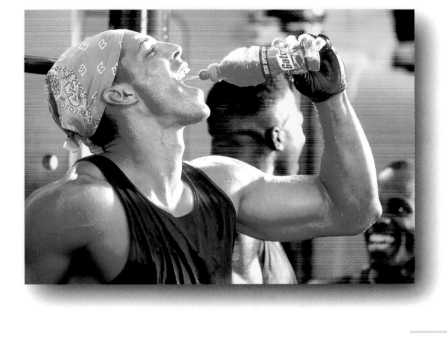

**PHOTOGRAPHER**
Carl Schneider

**DIGITAL CREATIVE**
Carl Schneider

**CLIENT**
Gatorade

**SOFTWARE**
Adobe Photoshop

**CATEGORY**
Advertising

## BLUR

**PHOTOGRAPHER**
Caesar Lima

**DIGITAL CREATIVE**
Caesar Lima

**CLIENT**
Alpinestars, Italy

**SOFTWARE**
Adobe Photoshop

**CATEGORY**
Sports

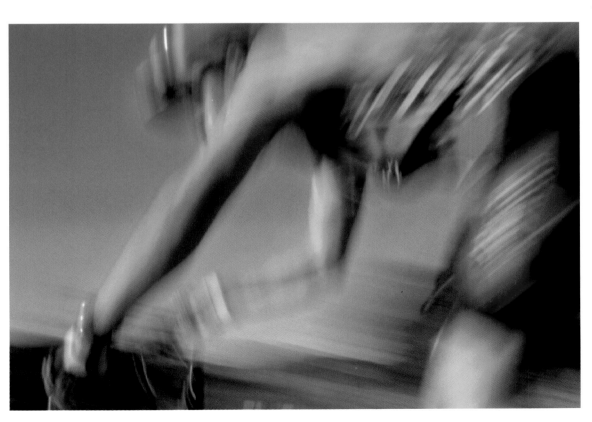

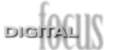

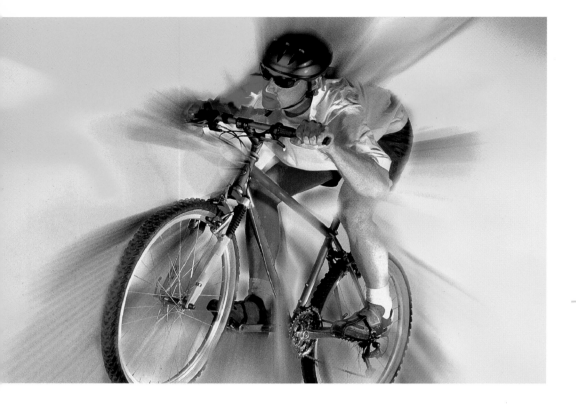

## BIKE RIDER

*PHOTOGRAPHER*
Ken Davies

*DIGITAL CREATIVE*
Ken Davies

*CLIENT*
Masterfile Photo Library

*SOFTWARE*
Adobe Photoshop

*CATEGORY*
Sports

## FAST BIKER

*PHOTOGRAPHER*
Caesar Lima

*DIGITAL CREATIVE*
Caesar Lima

*CLIENT*
Axion

*SOFTWARE*
Adobe Photoshop,
Specular Collage

*CATEGORY*
Advertising

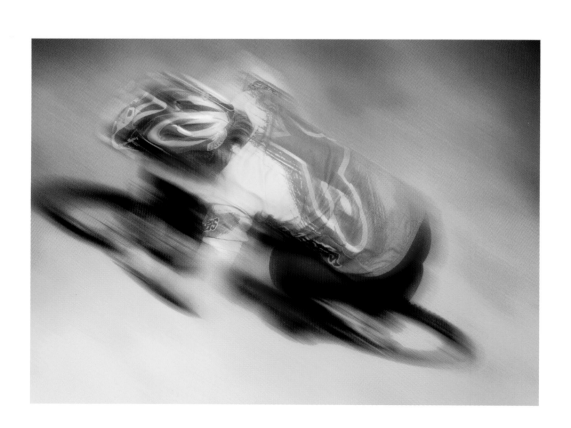

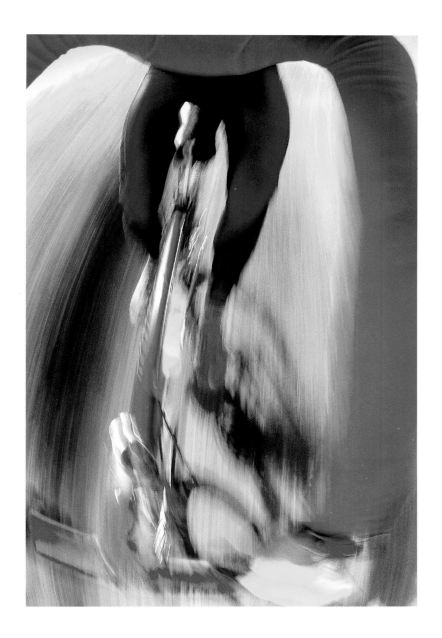

## MOUNTAIN BIKER'S EYE VIEW

*PHOTOGRAPHER*
Carl Schneider

*DIGITAL CREATIVE*
Carl Schneider

*CLIENT*
Kaiser Permanente

*SOFTWARE*
Adobe Photoshop

*CATEGORY*
Sports

## RUNNING FIGURE

*PHOTOGRAPHER*
Tom Collicott

*DIGITAL CREATIVE*
Tom Collicott

*CLIENT*
Adobe Magazine

*SOFTWARE*
Adobe Photoshop

*CATEGORY*
Editorial

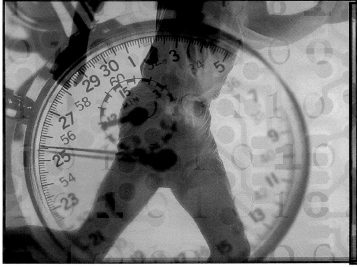

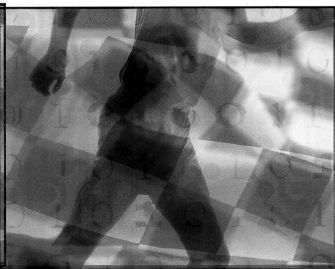

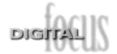

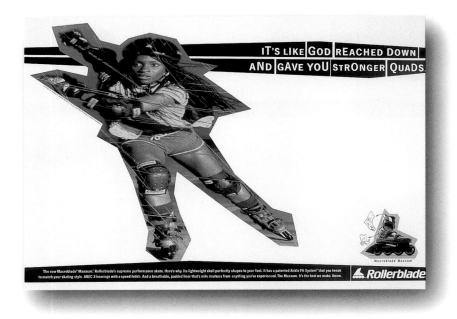

**IT'S LIKE GOD REACHED DOWN AND GAVE YOU STRONGER QUADS.**

The new Macroblade® Maxxum® Rollerblade's supreme performance skate. Here's why. Its lightweight shell perfectly shapes to your foot. It has a patented Ankle Fit System® that you tweak to match your skating style. ABEC 3 bearings with a speed fetish. And a breathable, padded liner that's mile markers from anything you've experienced. The Maxxum. It's the best we make. Amen.

**Rollerblade**

### ROLLERBLADE NATIONAL AD #1

*PHOTOGRAPHER*
**Carl Schneider**

*DIGITAL CREATIVE*
**Carl Schneider**

*CLIENT*
**Rollerblade**

*SOFTWARE*
**Adobe Photoshop**

*CATEGORY*
**Advertising**

**QUIT BRAKING LIKE FRED FLINTSTONE.**

The Rollerblade® ABT® brake brings stopping to the 21st century. Your foot goes forward. Brake goes down. You stop. All eight wheels stay on the ground. That means better control and balance. So go ahead. Test-stop the brake Inline Retailer named the "Best Technological Advancement of '94." B.C. or A.D.

**Rollerblade**

### ROLLERBLADE NATIONAL AD #2

*PHOTOGRAPHER*
**Carl Schneider**

*DIGITAL CREATIVE*
**Carl Schneider**

*CLIENT*
**Rollerblade**

*SOFTWARE*
**Adobe Photoshop**

*CATEGORY*
**Advertising**

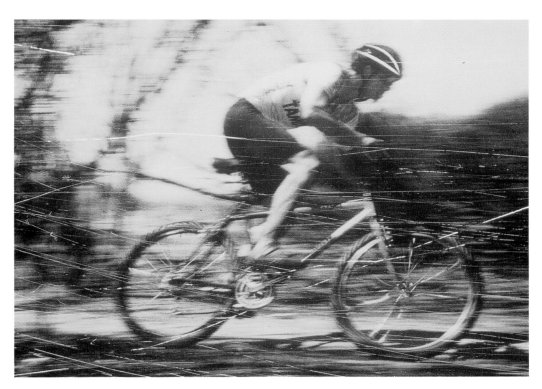

### SCRATCHED MOUNTAIN BIKER

*PHOTOGRAPHER*
**Carl Schneider**

*DIGITAL CREATIVE*
**Carl Schneider**

*CLIENT*
**Stock**

*SOFTWARE*
**Adobe Photoshop**

*CATEGORY*
**Sports**

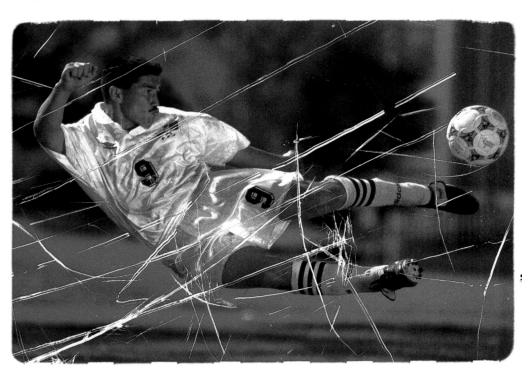

### SCRATCHED SOCCER

*PHOTOGRAPHER*
**Carl Schneider**

*DIGITAL CREATIVE*
**Carl Schneider**

*CLIENT*
**Miller Genuine Draft**

*SOFTWARE*
**Adobe Photoshop**

*CATEGORY*
**Sports**

SPORTS Sports

BUSINESS
business

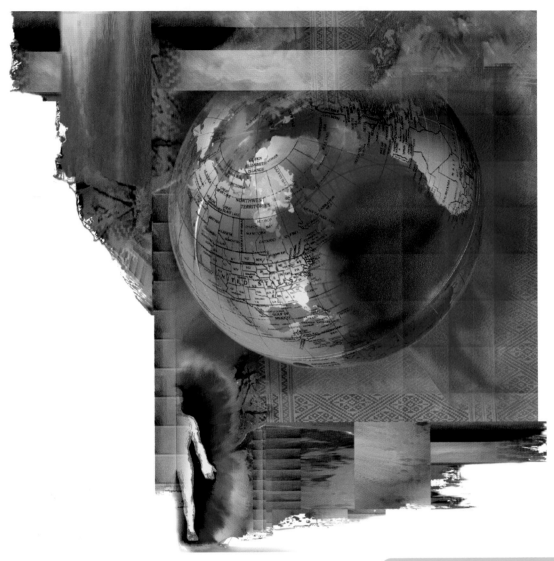

GLOBE WITH MAN

**GLOBE WITH MAN**

*PHOTOGRAPHER*
**Bob Schlowsky**

*DIGITAL CREATIVE*
**Lois Schlowsky**

*SOFTWARE*
**QFX, Adobe Photoshop**

*CATEGORY*
**Stock Digital Illustration**

# BOB & LOIS
# SCHLOWSKY

**Bob and Lois Schlowsky** produced this photograph for Tony Stone Images as a stock image. In this thoughtful expression of the relationship between the individual and the global community, they incorporate textural patterns from many different cultures. This richly layered and strikingly colorful piece suggests both the complexity and organic qualities of human experience.

**To** achieve this design, a variety of techniques was integrated and adapted from both traditional photo and digital technology. Colored gels were used to enhance the effects of the photography. Various elements were handpainted to soften the mood, and actual fabrics were scanned to acquire textures. Both QFX and Adobe Photoshop were implemented to assemble and finalize the image.

**Digital** technology is utilized to expand their creative options, while retaining a photographic and painterly sense. This uninhibited approach allows rough edges, textures and colors to blend with concepts to achieve a satisfying result.

41

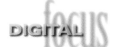 

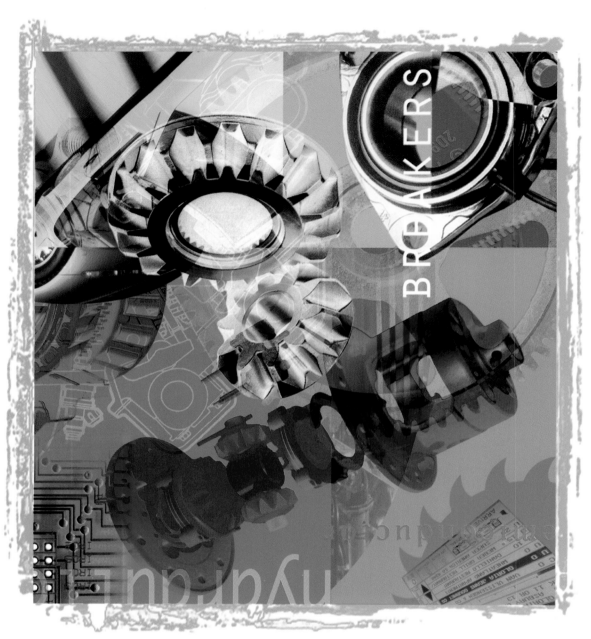

# ERIC YANG

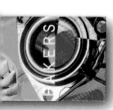

**Automotive Society for Quality Control Magazine** needed a contemporary illustration highlighting the new distinction in manufactured automobile parts. The premise was to depict actual elements in a very sophisticated style representing quality control.

**Photographs** and diagrams were scanned in Photoshop and special filters were applied to the images. They were then assembled in layers to form a combined collage effect. Multiple backgrounds, intersected by elements of type, were linked together to create the final illustration.

**The** colorful interaction of digital manipulation and ordinary parts is connected to form a provocative design. This intriguing high-tech illustration reflects the latest advancements in manufactured automobile parts. Eric Yang's fresh approach is typical of his unique ability to transform a traditional subject into an effective and meaningful image.

**ASQC**

*DIGITAL CREATIVE*
**Eric Yang**

*CLIENT*
**Automobile Society for Quality Control**

*SOFTWARE*
**Adobe Photoshop**

*CATEGORY*
**Business**

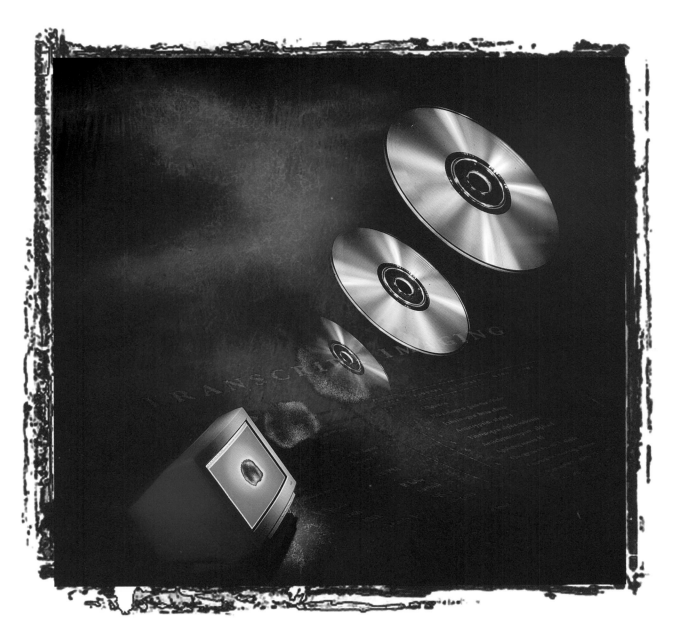

# GEOFFREY NELSON

**In** this advertisement depicting CD Disk Transcript Imaging software, Geoffrey Nelson brings clarity and understanding to a highly complicated scientific product. Using concise imagery, he visually describes the process of deciphering and decoding the most complex computer code — human DNA. The power of the product is forcefully accentuated by a surreal and almost magical background.

**Photographic** components were scanned and brought into Adobe Photoshop. The cell image on the computer screen was given the illusion of morphing into the CD-ROM through the use of scale, careful filtration, and blending. Color values and luminance were selected to focus attention. The text elements were then adjusted to display a subliminal effect.

**This** simple elaboration offers a clear illustration of an important medical research tool. With his precise style, Nelson clearly presents the integration of data, visual information and the latest in technology.

*PHOTOGRAPHER*
**Geoffrey Nelson**

*DIGITAL CREATIVE*
**Hausman Design**

*CLIENT*
**INCYTE**

*SOFTWARE*
**Adobe Photoshop**

*CATEGORY*
**Business**

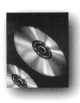

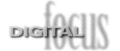 

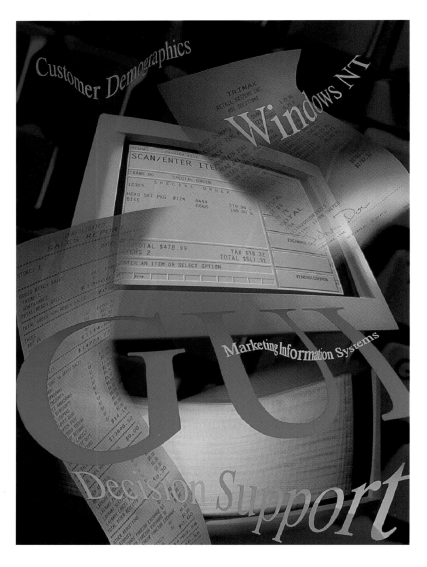

**GUI**

*PHOTOGRAPHER*
Ken Davies

*DIGITAL CREATIVE*
Ken Davies

*CLIENT*
Trimax Retail Systems

*SOFTWARE*
Adobe Photoshop

*CATEGORY*
Business

**APPLIED INTELLIGENCE COVER**

*ILLUSTRATOR*
Jeff Brice

*CLIENT*
Stewart Monderer Design

*SOFTWARE*
Adobe Photoshop,
Specular Collage

*CATEGORY*
Business

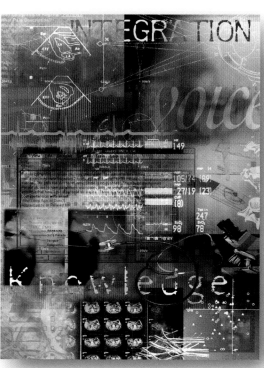

BUSINESS

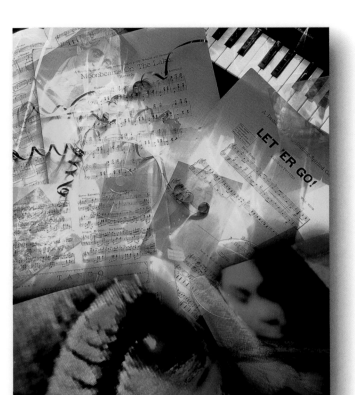

## MUSIC PUBLICATION COVER

*PHOTOGRAPHER*
**Ken Davies**

*DIGITAL CREATIVE*
**Ken Davies**

*CLIENT*
**Ink-Colour Expert**

*SOFTWARE*
**Adobe Photoshop**

*CATEGORY*
**Business**

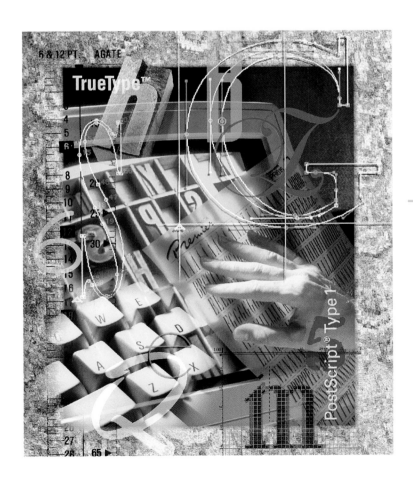

## FONTEK PACKAGING ART

*PHOTOGRAPHER*
**Dan Marcolina**

*DIGITAL CREATIVE*
**Dan Marcolina**

*CLIENT*
**Letraset**

*SOFTWARE*
**Color Studio**

*CATEGORY*
**Packaging**

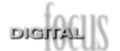

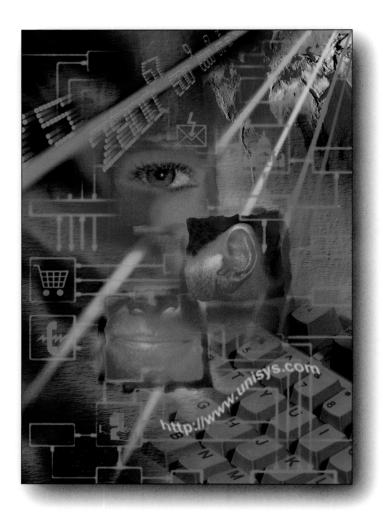

## ELECTRONIC COMMERCE

*PHOTOGRAPHER*
William Whitehurst

*DIGITAL CREATIVE*
William Whitehurst

*CLIENT*
Unisys

*SOFTWARE*
Adobe Photoshop, Live Picture

*CATEGORY*
Corporate Brochure

## INTERNET KEYS

*PHOTOGRAPHER*
William Whitehurst

*DIGITAL CREATIVE*
William Whitehurst

*CLIENT*
TSM

*SOFTWARE*
Adobe Photoshop

*CATEGORY*
Business

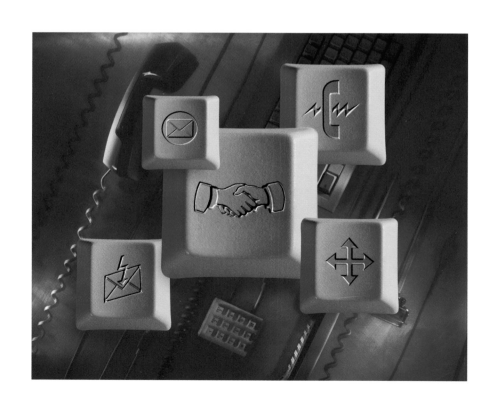

BUSINESS

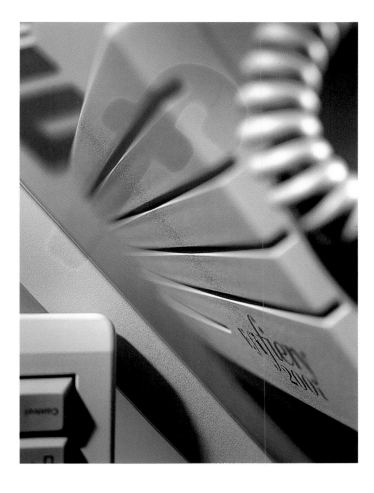

**EFI-FIREY 200I**

PHOTOGRAPHER
Stan Musilek

DIGITAL CREATIVE
Stan Musilek

CLIENT
EFI

SOFTWARE
Live Pictures

CATEGORY
Advertising

## PROGRAMMER

PHOTOGRAPHER
Bob Schlowsky

DIGITAL CREATIVE
Lois Schlowsky

CLIENT
Tony Stone Images

SOFTWARE
QFX, Adobe Photoshop

CATEGORY
Stock Digital Illustration

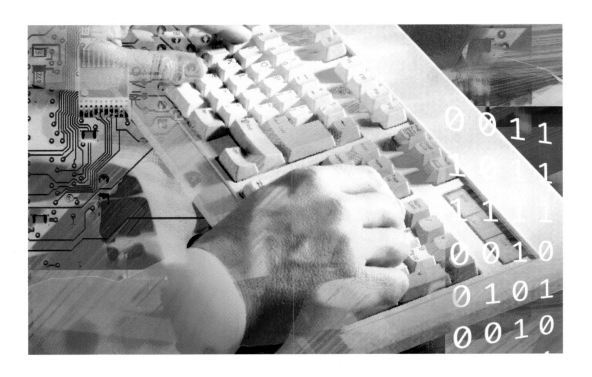

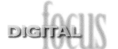

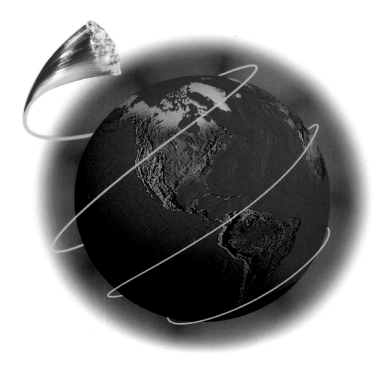

**FIBEROPTICS AROUND THE WORLD**

*PHOTOGRAPHER*
William Whitehurst

*DIGITAL CREATIVE*
William Whitehurst

*CLIENT*
TSM

*SOFTWARE*
Adobe Photoshop,
Live Picture,
Strata Studio Pro

*CATEGORY*
Business

**GLOBE & HAND**

*PHOTOGRAPHER*
Geoffrey Nelson

*DIGITAL CREATIVE*
Janet Brockett/Elements

*CLIENT*
Applied Materials

*SOFTWARE*
Adobe Photoshop

*CATEGORY*
Business

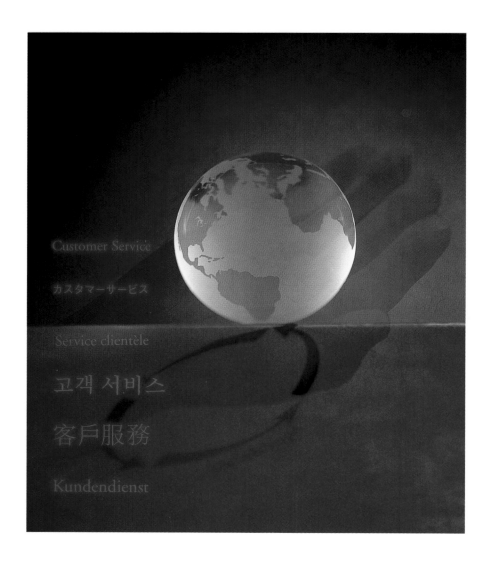

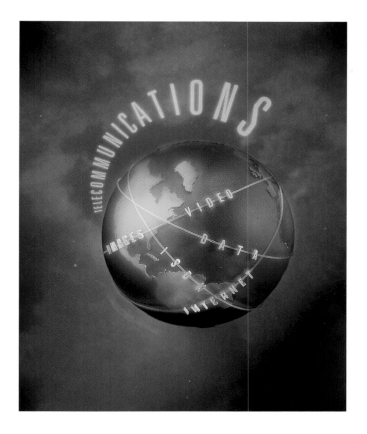

### GLOBE TELECOMMUNICATIONS

*PHOTOGRAPHER*
**Geoffrey Nelson**

*DIGITAL CREATIVE*
**Gordon Mortensen**

*CLIENT*
**Uniphase**

*SOFTWARE*
**Adobe Photoshop**

*CATEGORY*
**Business**

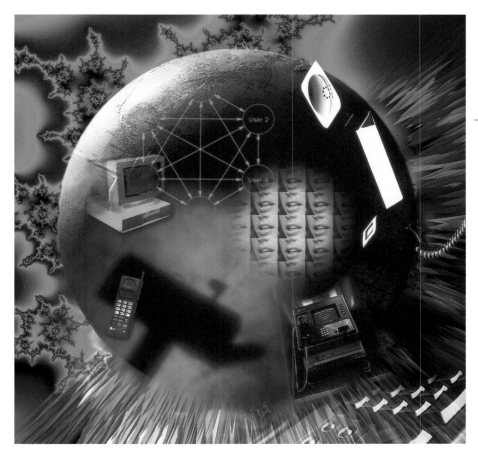

### TELECOMMUNICATIONS GLOBE

*PHOTOGRAPHER*
**Bill Milne**

*DIGITAL CREATIVE*
**Bill Milne**

*CLIENT*
**AT&T**

*SOFTWARE*
**Adobe Photoshop**

*CATEGORY*
**Advertising**

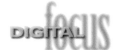

### TELECOMMUNICATIONS

*PHOTOGRAPHER*
**William Whitehurst**

*DIGITAL CREATIVE*
**William Whitehurst**

*CLIENT*
**Helicon**

*SOFTWARE*
**Adobe Photoshop, Live Picture**

*CATEGORY*
**Business**

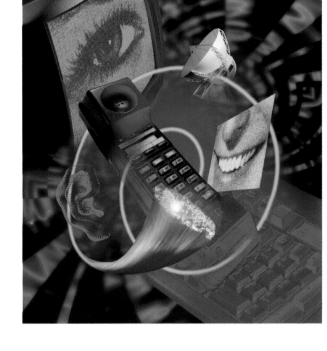

### VOICE VIDEO IMAGE

*PHOTOGRAPHER*
**Dan Marcolina, Stock**

*DIGITAL CREATIVE*
**Dan Marcolina**

*CLIENT*
**GTE Corporation**

*SOFTWARE*
**Adobe Photoshop, Specular Collage**

*CATEGORY*
**Business**

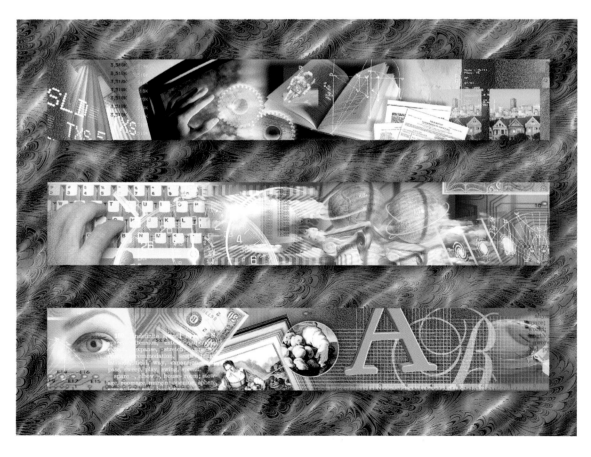

## IDEA

*PHOTOGRAPHER*

*DIGITAL CREATIVE*
Eric Yang

*CLIENT*
**U.S. Postal Service**

*SOFTWARE*
**Adobe Photoshop**

*CATEGORY*
**Government**

## PRIORITY MAIL

*DIGITAL CREATIVE*
Eric Yang

*CLIENT*
**U.S. Postal Service**

*SOFTWARE*
**Adobe Photoshop**

*CATEGORY*
**Government**

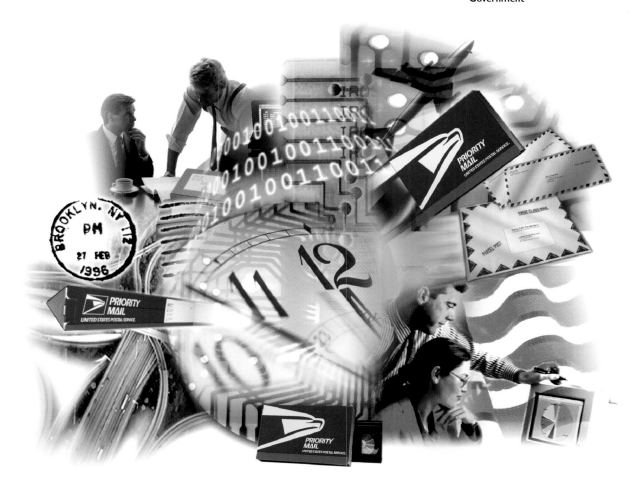

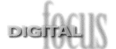

## HEAD MULTIDIMENSIONAL

*PHOTOGRAPHER*
**Geoffrey Nelson**

*DIGITAL CREATIVE*
**Ann Sison/1185 Design**

*CLIENT*
**Informix**

*SOFTWARE*
**Adobe Photoshop**

*CATEGORY*
**Business**

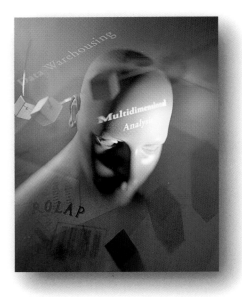

## HEAD PLANE, REFLECTIVE SPHERE

*PHOTOGRAPHER*
**Geoffrey Nelson**

*DIGITAL CREATIVE*
**Vernon Head/VGB**

*CLIENT*
**Phillips**

*SOFTWARE*
**Adobe Photoshop**

*CATEGORY*
**Business**

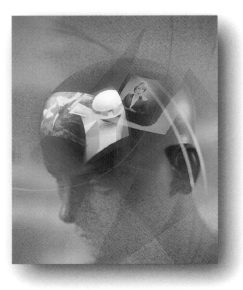

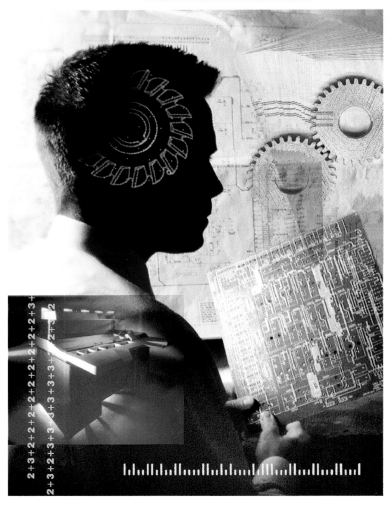

## OPEX

*PHOTOGRAPHER*
**Dan Marcolina**

*DIGITAL CREATIVE*
**Dan Marcolina**

*CLIENT*
**Opex**

*SOFTWARE*
**Adobe Photoshop**

*CATEGORY*
**Business**

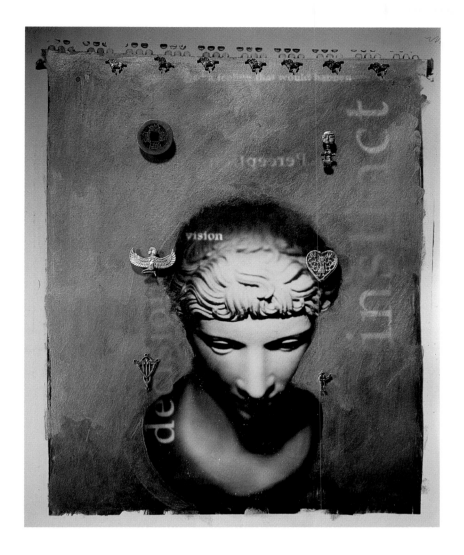

### SCULPTURE HEAD

*PHOTOGRAPHER*
**Geoffrey Nelson**

*DIGITAL CREATIVES*
**Rich Nelson, Mark Anderson Design**

*SOFTWARE*
**Adobe Photoshop**

*CATEGORY*
**Business**

### HEAD MULTIMEDIA

*PHOTOGRAPHER*
**Geoffrey Nelson**

*DIGITAL CREATIVE*
**Vernon Head/VGB**

*CLIENT*
**Phillips**

*SOFTWARE*
**Adobe Photoshop**

*CATEGORY*
**Business**

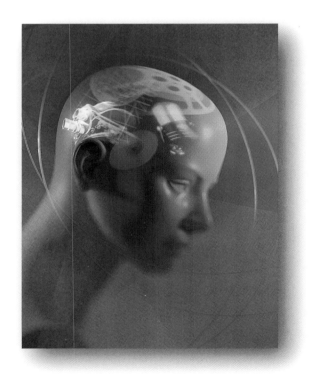

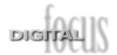

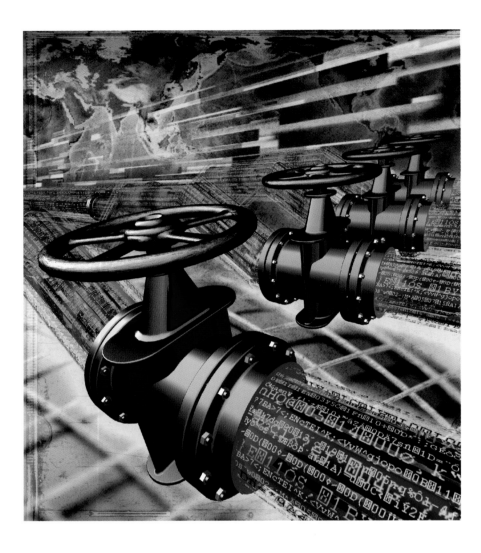

### DAT PIPE

*DIGITAL CREATIVE*
**Rob Magiera**

*CLIENT*
**Transcapacity**

*SOFTWARE*
**Adobe Photoshop,
Alias Power Animator**

*CATEGORY*
**Corporate**

### MAP PIPE

*DIGITAL CREATIVE*
**Rob Magiera**

*CLIENT*
**Transcapacity**

*SOFTWARE*
**Adobe Photoshop,
Alias Power Animator**

*CATEGORY*
**Corporate**

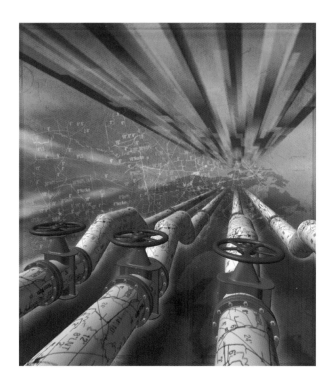

## MAN AT COMPUTER

*PHOTOGRAPHER*
Ken Davies

*DIGITAL CREATIVE*
Ken Davies

*CLIENT*
ATI

*SOFTWARE*
Adobe Photoshop

*CATEGORY*
Annual Report

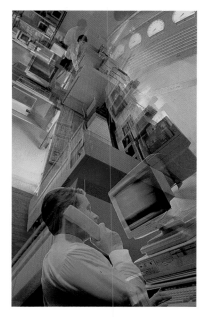

## NETWORKING

*PHOTOGRAPHER*
Bill Milne

*DIGITAL CREATIVE*
Bill Milne

*CLIENT*
AT&T

*SOFTWARE*
Adobe Photoshop

*CATEGORY*
Advertising

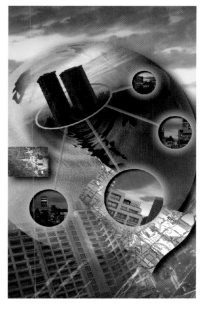

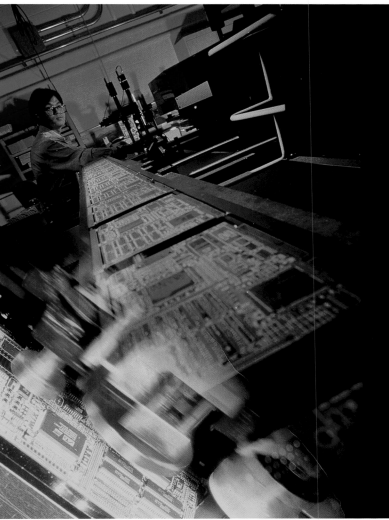

## CIRCUIT BOARD VIEWPOINT

*PHOTOGRAPHER*
Ken Davies

*DIGITAL CREATIVE*
Ken Davies

*CLIENT*
ATI

*SOFTWARE*
Adobe Photoshop

*CATEGORY*
Business

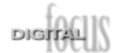

## ELECTRIC COMMERCE

*DIGITAL CREATIVE*
Eric Yang

*CLIENT*
Computer Science Corporation

*SOFTWARE*
Adobe Photoshop

*CATEGORY*
Corporate Brochure

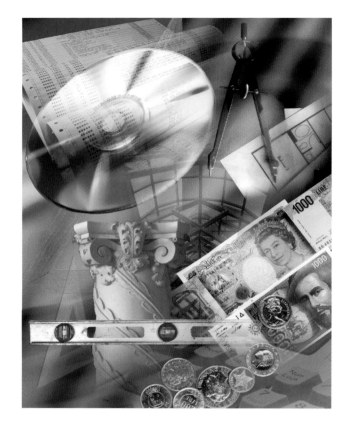

## WILMINGTON TRUST ANNUAL REPORT

*PHOTOGRAPHER*
Dan Marcolina/Video

*DIGITAL CREATIVE*
Dan Marcolina

*CLIENT*
Wilmington Trust

*SOFTWARE*
Video Capture, Adobe Photoshop

*CATEGORY*
Annual Report

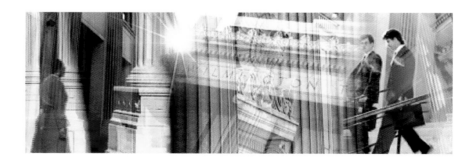

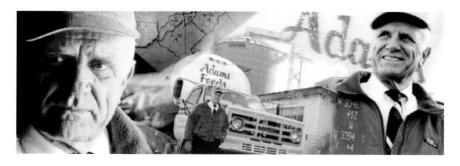

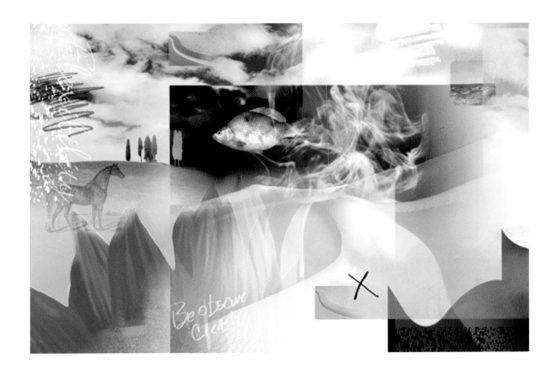

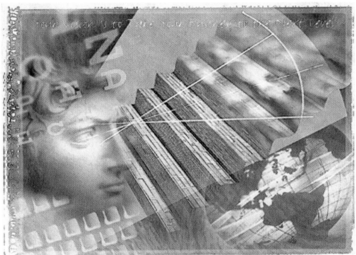

## ITC DESIGN PALLET

**PHOTOGRAPHER**
Various

**DIGITAL CREATIVE**
Dan Marcolina

**CLIENT**
International Typeface Corporation

**SOFTWARE**
Adobe Photoshop, Specular Collage

**CATEGORY**
Business

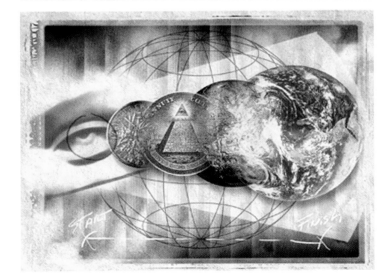

## BRINGING YOUR VISION TO THE NEXT LEVEL

**DIGITAL CREATIVE**
Dan Marcolina

**CLIENT**
Sun Microsystems

**SOFTWARE**
Adobe Photoshop,
Specular Collage, Infini-D

**CATEGORY**
Business

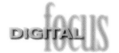

## VIRGIN GAMES COVER

*PHOTOGRAPHERS*
**Ronald Dunlap, Bill Brewer**

*DIGITAL CREATIVES*
**Ronald Dunlap, Tony Honkawa**

*CLIENT*
**Virgin Games**

*SOFTWARE*
**Adobe Photoshop**

*CATEGORY*
**Business**

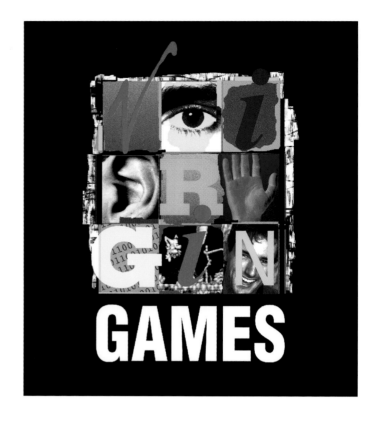

## TAWERET'S GAME

*PHOTOGRAPHER*
**Ronald Dunlap**

*DIGITAL CREATIVE*
**Ronald Dunlap**

*CLIENT*
**Dogbyte Development**

*SOFTWARE*
**Adobe Photoshop**

*CATEGORY*
**Business**

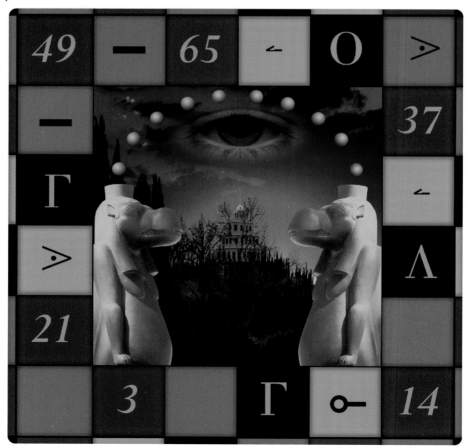

BUSINESS

**MOTION SOUND & VISION**

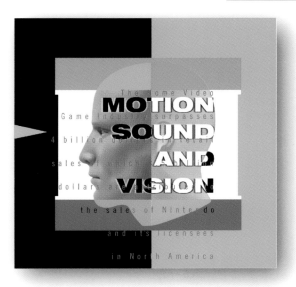

*PHOTOGRAPHER*
**Ronald Dunlap**

*DIGITAL CREATIVE*
**Ronald Dunlap**

*CLIENT*
**Virgin Games**

*SOFTWARE*
**Adobe Photoshop**

*CATEGORY*
**Business**

**VITAMIN PACKAGING**

*PHOTOGRAPHER*
**Bill Milne**

*DIGITAL CREATIVE*
**Bill Milne**

*CLIENT*
**Life Science Nutritional**

*SOFTWARE*
**Adobe Photoshop, Poser, Adobe Illustrator**

*CATEGORY*
**Advertising**

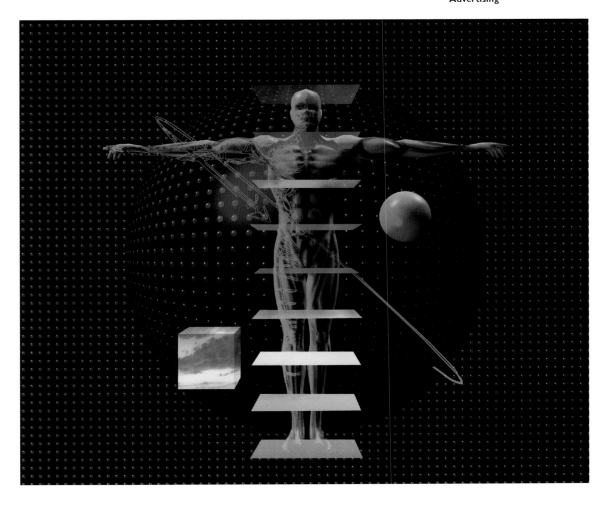

## COMPUTER MONITOR CALLER ID

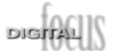

**PHOTOGRAPHER**
Geoffrey Nelson

**DIGITAL CREATIVE**
Marc Eis, Shugart/Matson

**CLIENT**
Pacific Bell

**SOFTWARE**
Adobe Photoshop

**CATEGORY**
Business

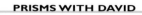

## PRISMS WITH DAVID

**PHOTOGRAPHER**
Bob Schlowsky

**DIGITAL CREATIVE**
Lois Schlowsky

**CLIENT**
Tony Stone Images

**SOFTWARE**
QFX, Adobe Photoshop

**CATEGORY**
Stock Digital Illustration

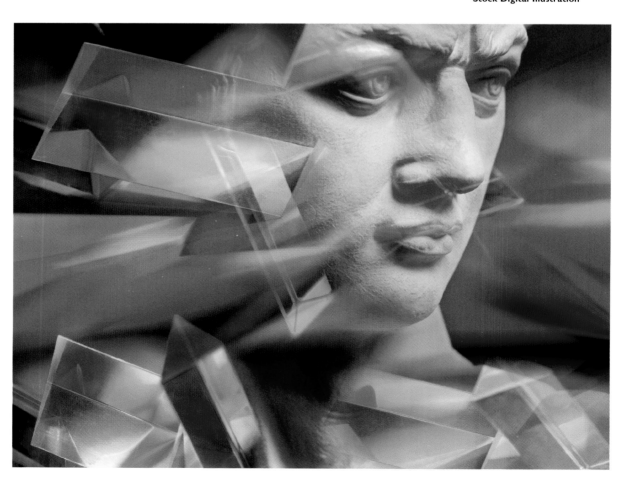

BUSINESS

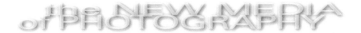

## HAND GLOBE

**PHOTOGRAPHER**
Geoffrey Nelson

**DIGITAL CREATIVE**
Rich Nelson/CKS

**SOFTWARE**
Adobe Photoshop

**CATEGORY**
Business

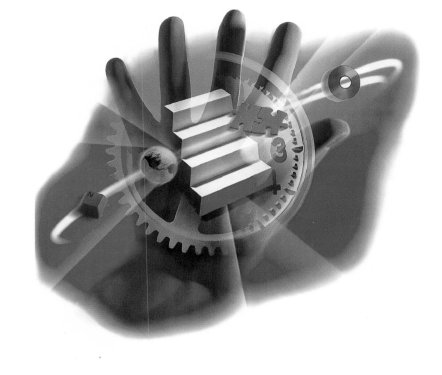

## INTERNATIONAL BANKING

**PHOTOGRAPHER**
Bob Schlowsky

**DIGITAL CREATIVE**
Lois Schlowsky

**CLIENT**
Tony Stone Images

**SOFTWARE**
QFX, Adobe Photoshop

**CATEGORY**
Stock Digital Illustration

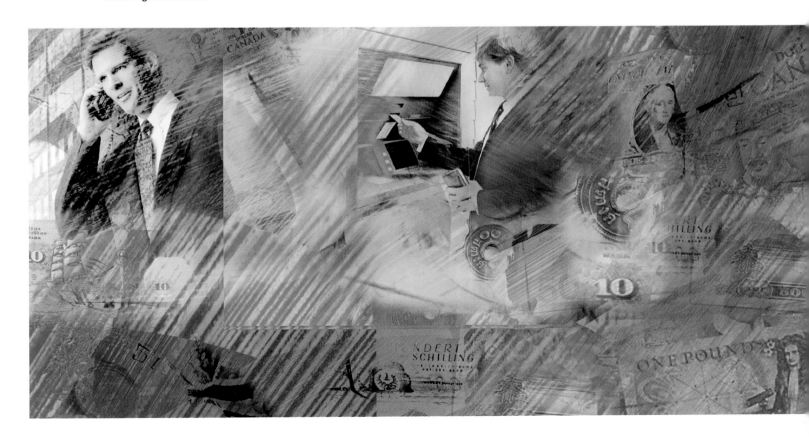

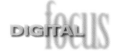

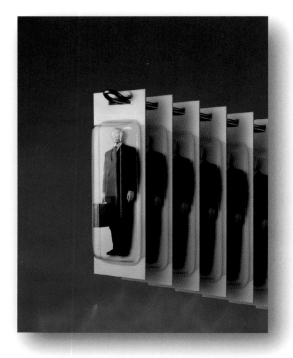

## PAK MAN

*PHOTOGRAPHER*
**Rick Dunn**

*DIGITAL CREATIVE*
**Rick Dunn**

*CLIENT*
**Brown Brothers, U.K.**

*SOFTWARE*
**Adobe Photoshop**

*CATEGORY*
**Advertising**

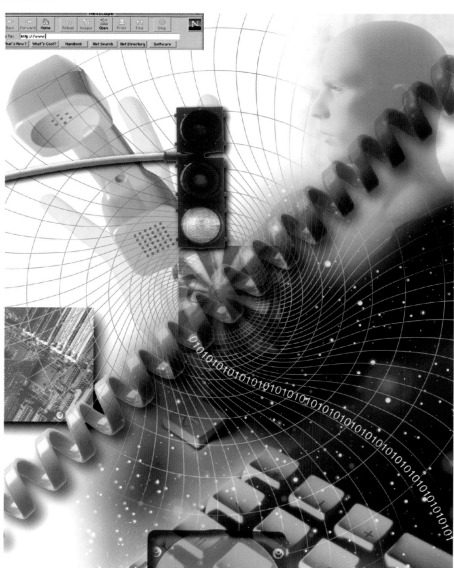

## WEB DESIGN/STOCK SHOT

*PHOTOGRAPHER*
**Bill Milne**

*DIGITAL CREATIVE*
**Bill Milne**

*CLIENT*
**AT&T**

*SOFTWARE*
**Adobe Photoshop**

*CATEGORY*
**Business Publication**

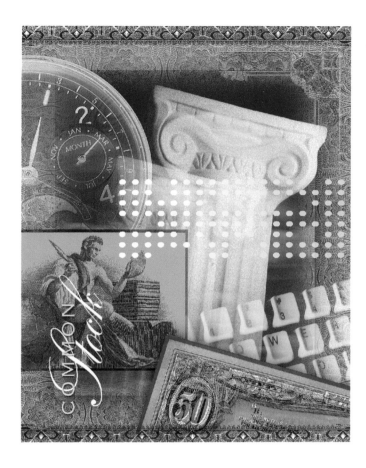

**DEAN WITTER COMMON STOCK**

*DIGITAL CREATIVE*
Dan Marcolina

*CLIENT*
Dean Witter

*SOFTWARE*
Adobe Photoshop

*CATEGORY*
Business

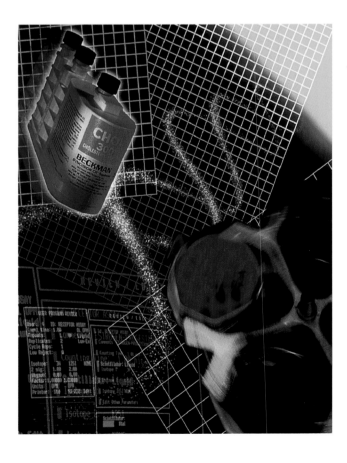

**CHOL 300**

*DIGITAL CREATIVES*
Shelly Beck, Tim Alt

*CLIENT*
Beckman Industries

*SOFTWARE*
Adobe Photoshop

*CATEGORY*
Business

**Business** *business*

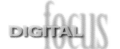

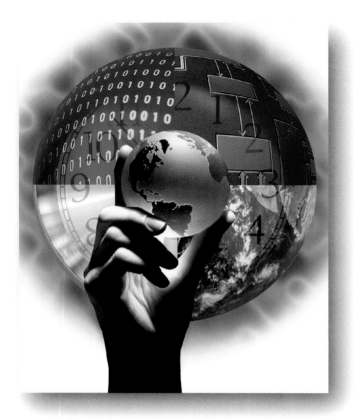

## WORLD IN HAND

*PHOTOGRAPHER*
**William Whitehurst**

*DIGITAL CREATIVE*
**William Whitehurst**

*CLIENT*
**TSM**

*SOFTWARE*
**Adobe Photoshop, Live
Picture**

*CATEGORY*
**Business**

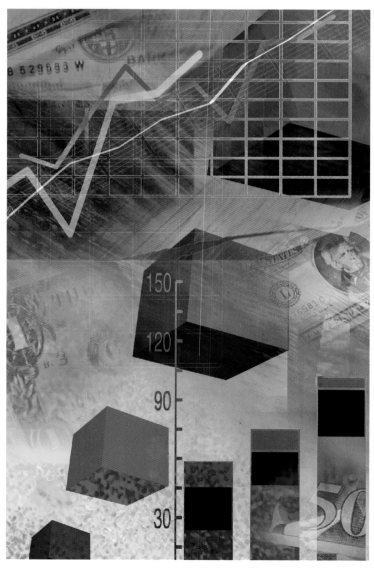

## CUBES & MONEY

*PHOTOGRAPHER*
**Bob Schlowsky, Stock Images**

*DIGITAL CREATIVE*
**Lois Schlowsky**

*CLIENT*
**State Street Bank**

*SOFTWARE*
**QFX, Adobe Photoshop**

*CATEGORY*
**Business, Promotion**

BUSINESS

## FINANCIAL COLLAGE

*PHOTOGRAPHER*
**William Whitehurst**

*DIGITAL CREATIVE*
**William Whitehurst**

*CLIENT*
**TSM**

*SOFTWARE*
**Adobe Photoshop,
Specular Collage**

*CATEGORY*
**Business**

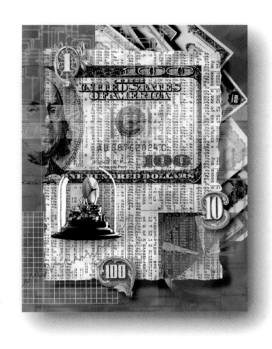

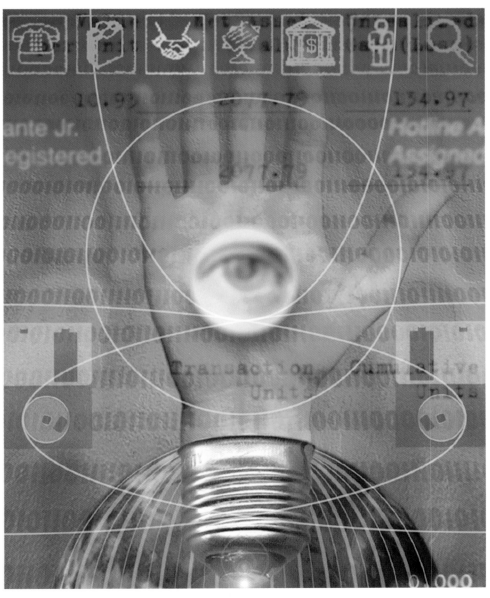

## BUSCIPLINE

*PHOTOGRAPHER*
**Paul Watson**

*DIGITAL CREATIVE*
**Paul Watson**

*CLIENT*
**Financial Planning Magazine**

*SOFTWARE*
**Adobe Photoshop**

*CATEGORY*
**Business**

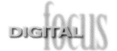

## RESPONSECALL

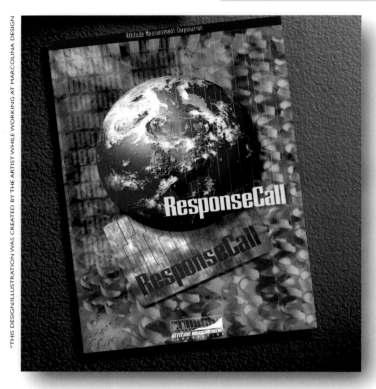

*THIS DESIGN/ILLUSTRATION WAS CREATED BY THE ARTIST WHILE WORKING AT MARCOLINA DESIGN

**DIGITAL CREATIVE**
Matthew Peacock*
Anonymous Productions

**CLIENT**
Attitude Measurement Corporation

**SOFTWARE**
Adobe Photoshop, Adobe Illustrator

**CATEGORY**
Business

## AIRPLANES

**PHOTOGRAPHER**
Bob Schlowsky

**DIGITAL**

**CREATIVE**
Lois Schlowsky

**CLIENT**
RasterOps Annual
Report

**SOFTWARE**
QFX, Adobe
Photoshop

**CATEGORY**
Annual Report Cover

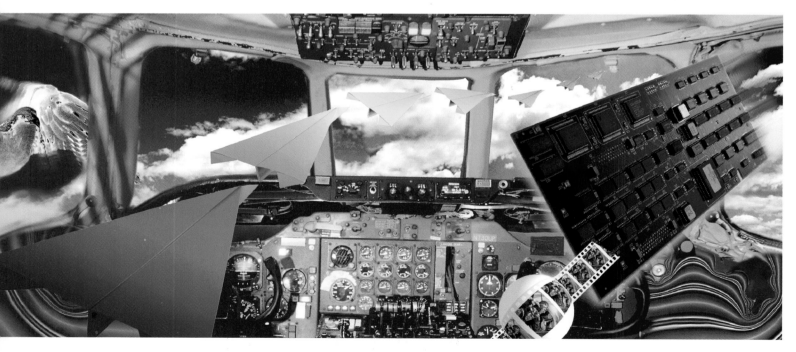

BUSINESS

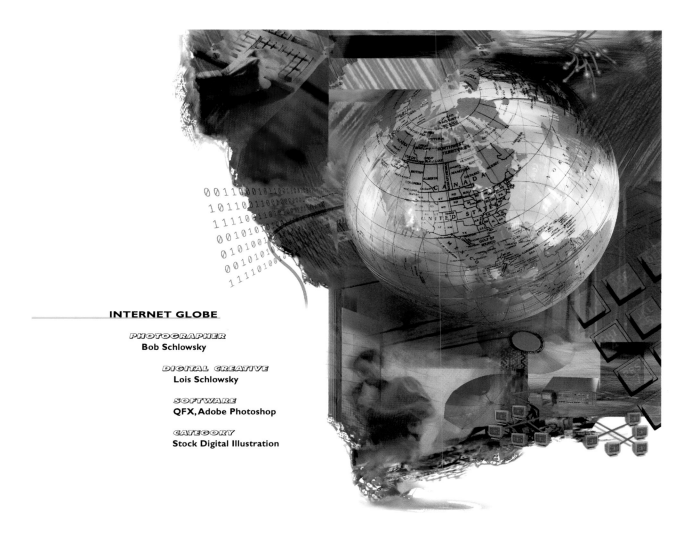

### INTERNET GLOBE

*PHOTOGRAPHER*
**Bob Schlowsky**

*DIGITAL CREATIVE*
**Lois Schlowsky**

*SOFTWARE*
**QFX, Adobe Photoshop**

*CATEGORY*
**Stock Digital Illustration**

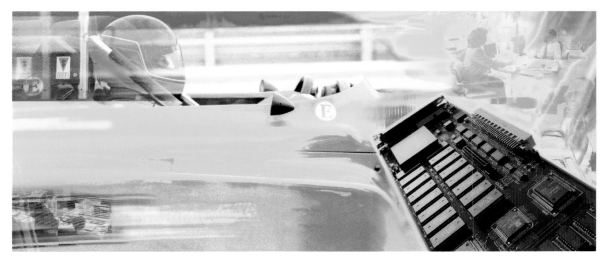

### RACE CAR IN BUSINESS

*PHOTOGRAPHER*
**Bob Schlowsky**

*DIGITAL CREATIVE*
**Lois Schlowsky**

*CLIENT*
**RasterOps Annual Report**

*SOFTWARE*
**QFX, Adobe Photoshop**

*CATEGORY*
**Annual Report Cover**

*people*

PEOPLE

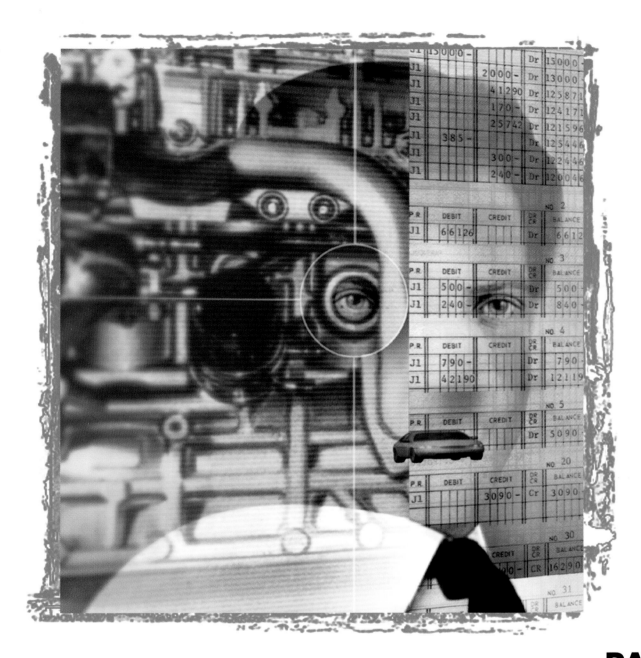

# WATSON **PAUL**

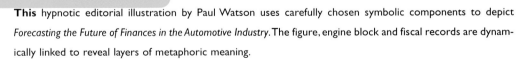

*PHOTOGRAPHER*
**Paul Watson**

*DIGITAL CREATIVE*
**Paul Watson**

*CLIENT*
**Mainstay Communications**

*SOFTWARE*
**Adobe Photoshop**

*CATEGORY*
**Editorial**

**This** hypnotic editorial illustration by Paul Watson uses carefully chosen symbolic components to depict *Forecasting the Future of Finances in the Automotive Industry*. The figure, engine block and fiscal records are dynamically linked to reveal layers of metaphoric meaning.

**Photographic** transparencies of the various elements were scanned into Adobe Photoshop. They were then saved as individual layers with different degrees of opacity and the segments were juxtaposed to form a composition of asymmetric balance. Light and shadow were used to define and connect parts of the design. The contrast of a warm and cool color palette heighten the visual tension and impact of the illustration.

**Through** the subtle blending of key details and features, Watson is able to embed complex coded messages into seemingly simply visual structures. Working from his studio in Toronto, he uses the digital medium to create somewhat eerie and compelling effects and reveals uncommon and exciting design solutions.

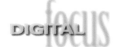
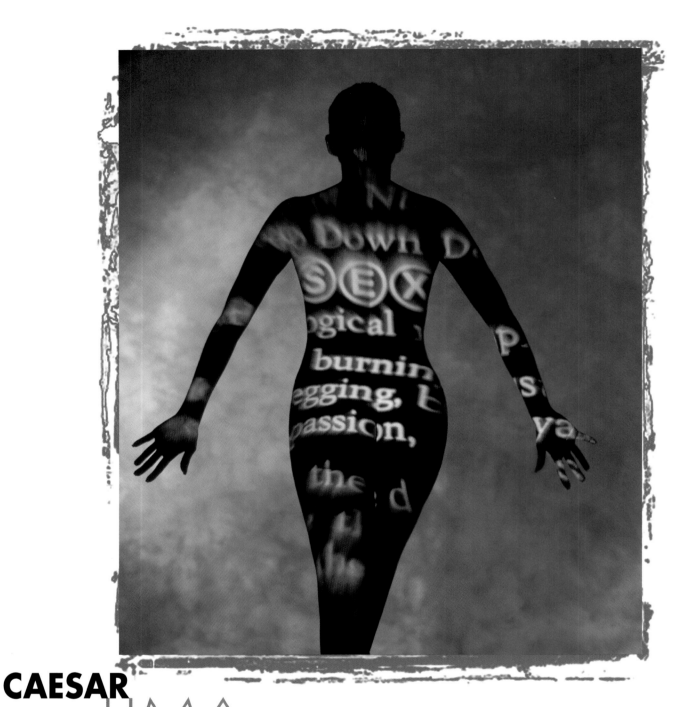

# CAESAR LIMA

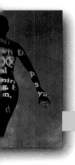

**Dramatic** and compelling, this image by Caesar Lima, of Caesar Photo Design, delivers an immediate message. Designed as a self-promotion, its meaning is conveyed by what is hidden and what is revealed. This provocative mood is captured and enhanced through the distorted words on the figure.

**In** constructing the image, traditional studio photography and digital manipulation techniques were combined in a unique way. Working in Adobe Illustrator and Photoshop, text elements were first developed and output in transparency form. The words were then projected on the silhouette shape of the model. The exact distance of the projection was critical in preventing it from appearing on the background. This striking use of light and language, depicted a subtle sense of illusion.

**Born** in Brazil, Caesar brings a unique, aesthetic slant to his work. Expanding the language of photography with digital manipulation, he pushes ideas to their limits—allowing mood and meaning to merge.

*PHOTOGRAPHER*
**Caesar Lima**

*DIGITAL CREATIVE*
**Caesar Lima**

*CLIENT*
**Caesar Photo Design, Inc.**

*SOFTWARE*
**Adobe Photoshop**

*CATEGORY*
**Self Promotion/Editorial**

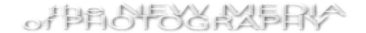
## FOUR FASHION FIGURES

*PHOTOGRAPHER*
Stan Musilek

*DIGITAL CREATIVE*
Stan Musilek

*CLIENT*
Vidal Sassoon

*SOFTWARE*
Live Pictures

*CATEGORY*
Advertising

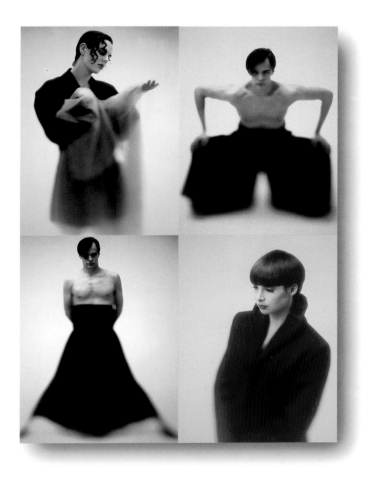

## THE GIFT

*PHOTOGRAPHERS*
Sharon White/Bob Packert

*DIGITAL CREATIVES*
Sharon White/Bob Packert

*CLIENT*
White/Packert

*SOFTWARE*
Adobe Photoshop

*CATEGORY*
Christmas Card

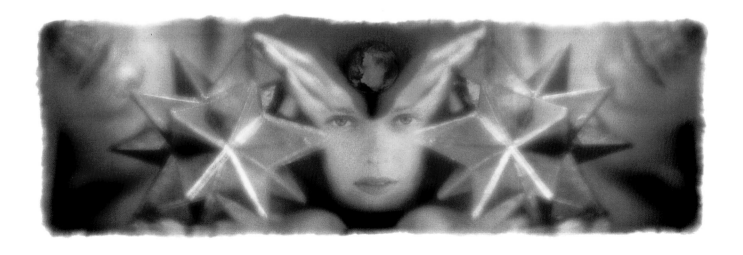

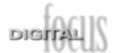

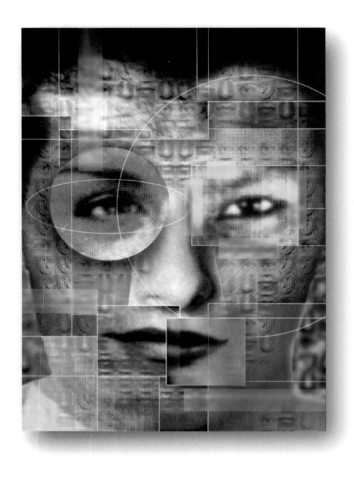

## FACETED

*PHOTOGRAPHER*
**Paul Watson**

*DIGITAL CREATIVE*
**Paul Watson**

*CLIENT*
**Physicians Management**

*SOFTWARE*
**Adobe Photoshop**

*CATEGORY*
**Editorial**

## BYTOWN EVOLUTE

*PHOTOGRAPHER*
**Paul Watson**

*DIGITAL CREATIVE*
**Paul Watson**

*CLIENT*
**The Bytown Group**

*SOFTWARE*
**Adobe Photoshop**

*CATEGORY*
**Advertising**

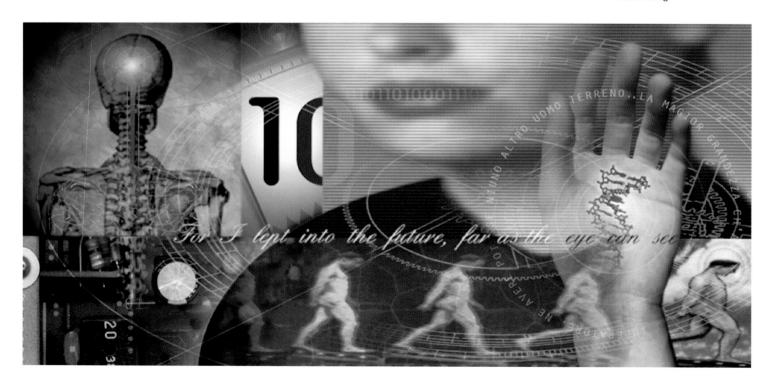

### EVOL

**PHOTOGRAPHER**
Paul Watson

**DIGITAL CREATIVE**
Paul Watson

**CLIENT**
Equinox

**SOFTWARE**
Adobe Photoshop

**CATEGORY**
Editorial

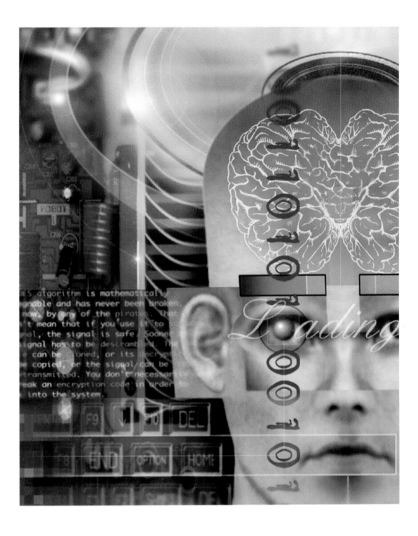

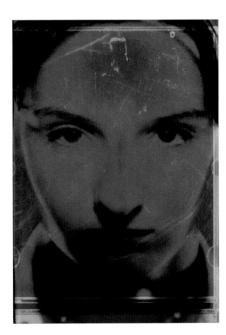

### BRITTANY

**PHOTOGRAPHER**
Erik Osterling

**DIGITAL CREATIVE**
Rob Magiera

**CLIENT**
Personal

**SOFTWARE**
Adobe Photoshop

**CATEGORY**
Self Promotion

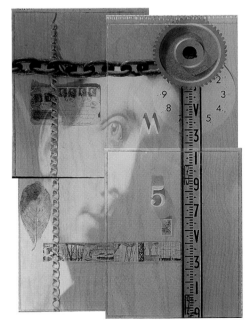

### SEPIA FACE

**PHOTOGRAPHER**
Tom Collicott

**DIGITAL CREATIVE**
Tom Collicott

**CLIENT**
Microsoft

**SOFTWARE**
Adobe Photoshop

**CATEGORY**
Advertising

*people*

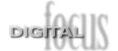
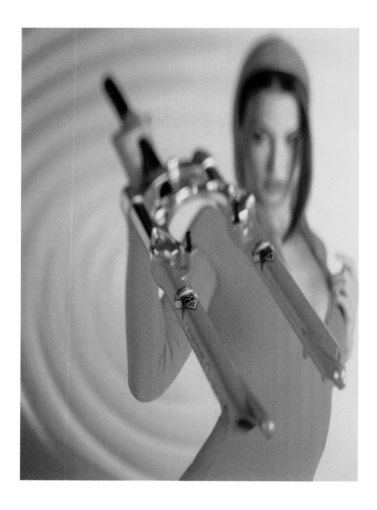

## ZOK GIRL

*PHOTOGRAPHER*
Caesar Lima

*DIGITAL CREATIVE*
Caesar Lima

*CLIENT*
Marzocchi, Italy

*SOFTWARE*
Adobe Photoshop

*CATEGORY*
Advertising

## MAN WITH COLLAR

*PHOTOGRAPHER*
Nick Koudis

*DIGITAL CREATIVE*
Koudis Nick

*CLIENT*
Comedy Central

*SOFTWARE*
Adobe Photoshop

*CATEGORY*
Advertising

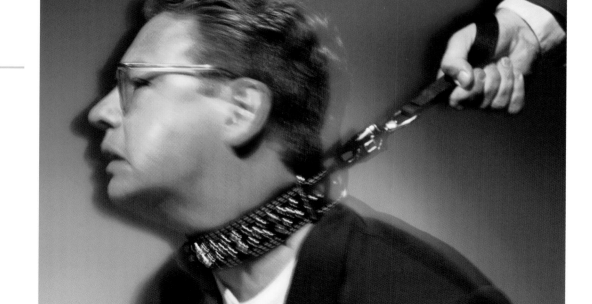

People People People

## FLYING LAPTOP

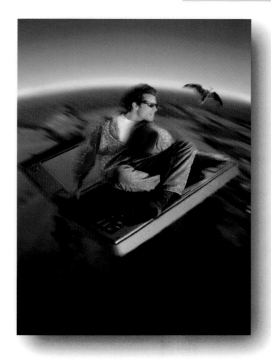

*PHOTOGRAPHER*
**Nick Koudis**

*DIGITAL CREATIVE*
**Koudis Nick**

*CLIENT*
**Internet World Magazine**

*SOFTWARE*
**Adobe Photoshop**

*CATEGORY*
**Editorial**

## WOMAN WITH FISH

*PHOTOGRAPHER*
**Ken Davies**

*DIGITAL CREATIVE*
**Ken Davies**

*CLIENT*
**Ink-Colour Expert**

*SOFTWARE*
**Adobe Photoshop**

*CATEGORY*
**Business**

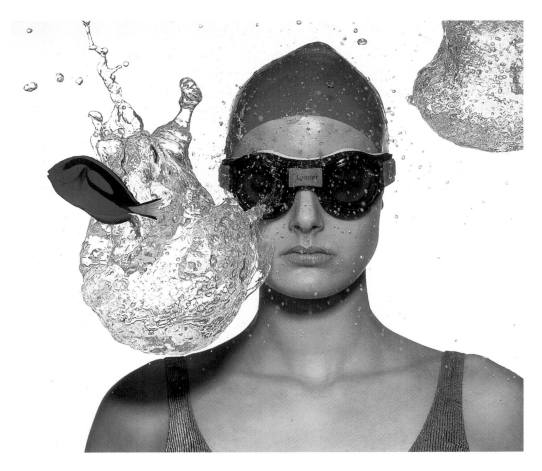

*people*

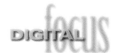

## THINKER

PHOTOGRAPHER
**Tim Alt**

DIGITAL CREATIVE
**Tim Alt**

SOFTWARE
**Electric Image**

CATEGORY
**Stock**

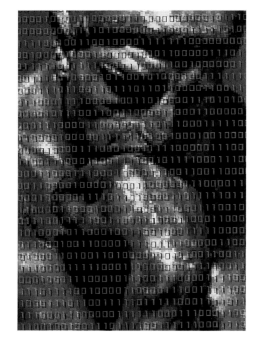

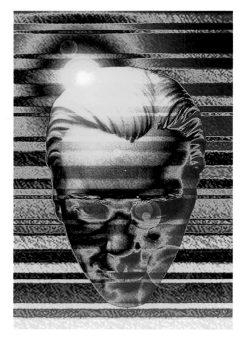

## HEAD WITH STRIPES

PHOTOGRAPHER
**Tim Alt**

DIGITAL CREATIVE
**Tim Alt**

SOFTWARE
**Photoshop, Texture Scape**

CATEGORY
**Stock**

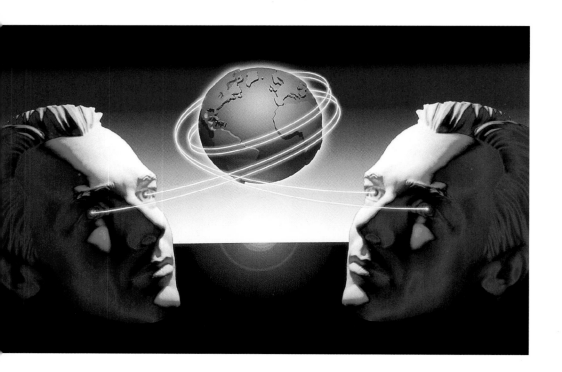

## TWO HEADS

PHOTOGRAPHER
**Tim Alt**

DIGITAL CREATIVE
**Tim Alt**

SOFTWARE
**Adobe Photoshop, Strata 3D,
Macromedia Freehand**

CATEGORY
**Stock**

People People People

## TOPOGRAPHICAL FACE

*PHOTOGRAPHER*
**Tim Alt**

*DIGITAL CREATIVE*
**Tim Alt**

*SOFTWARE*
**Electric Image**

*CATEGORY*
**Stock**

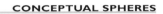

## CONCEPTUAL SPHERES

*PHOTOGRAPHER*
**Richard Wahlstrom**

*DIGITAL CREATIVE*
**Richard Wahlstrom**

*CLIENT*
**Ascend**

*SOFTWARE*
**Adobe Photoshop**

*CATEGORY*
**Advertising**

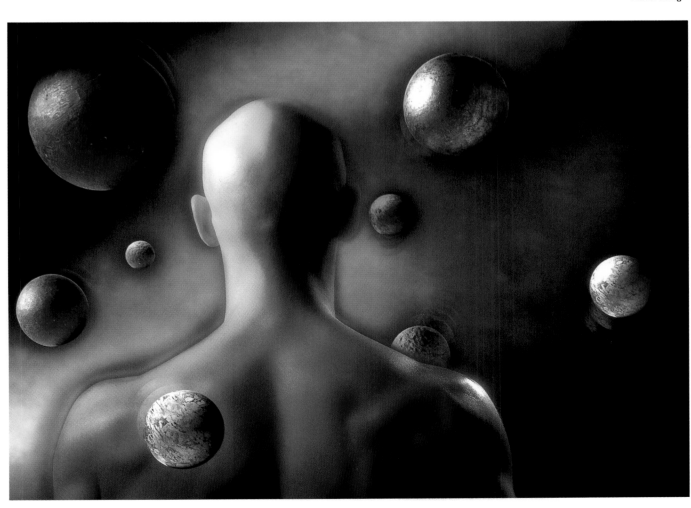

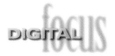

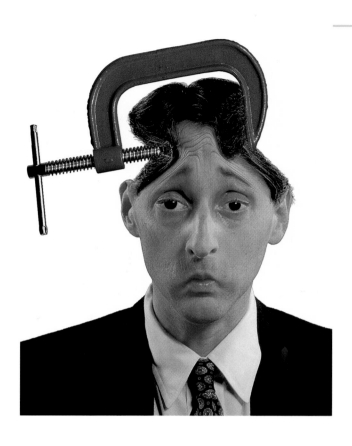

## VICE HEAD

**PHOTOGRAPHER**
Barry Blackman

**DIGITAL CREATIVE**
Barry Blackman

**CLIENT**
Rx

**SOFTWARE**
Barco Creator

**CATEGORY**
Promotion

## CRAZED JUDGE

**PHOTOGRAPHER**
J.W. Burkey

**DIGITAL CREATIVE**
J.W. Burkey

**CLIENT**
Stock Image

**SOFTWARE**
Adobe Photoshop

**CATEGORY**
Stock

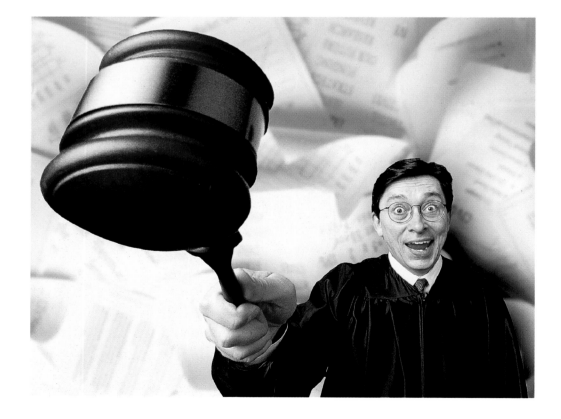

People

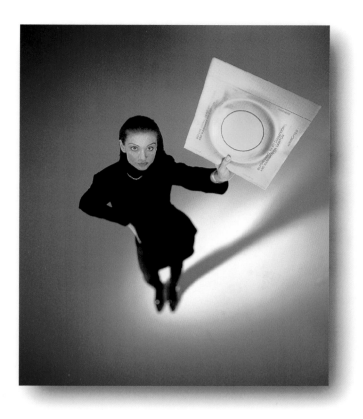

## CONDOM GIRL

*PHOTOGRAPHER*
Stan Musilek

*DIGITAL CREATIVE*
Stan Musilek

*CLIENT*
Stan Musilek

*SOFTWARE*
Live Pictures

*CATEGORY*
Self-Promotion

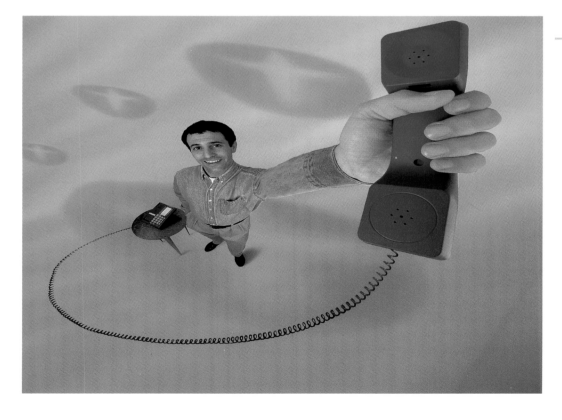

## MAN WITH PHONE

*PHOTOGRAPHER*
Ken Davies

*DIGITAL CREATIVE*
Ken Davies

*CLIENT*
Citibank

*SOFTWARE*
Adobe Photoshop

*CATEGORY*
Advertising

PEOPLE
*people*

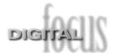

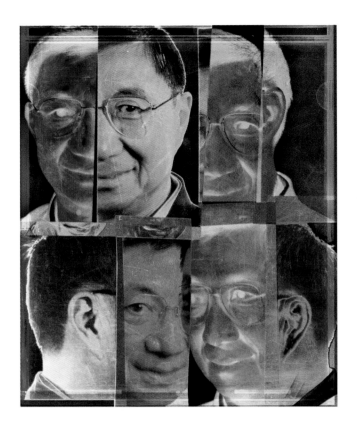

**PORTRAIT #3**

*PHOTOGRAPHER*
Daniel Arsnault

*DIGITAL CREATIVE*
Rob Magiera

*CLIENT*
Discovery Magazine

*SOFTWARE*
Adobe Photoshop

*CATEGORY*
Editorial

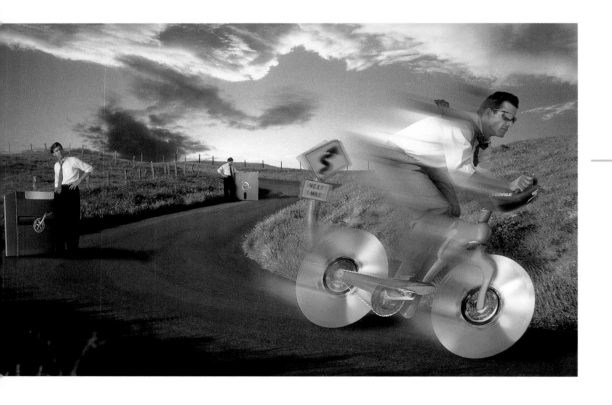

**BIKER**

*PHOTOGRAPHER*
Richard Wahlstrom

*DIGITAL CREATIVE*
Richard Wahlstrom

*CLIENT*
Sony

*SOFTWARE*
Adobe Photoshop

*CATEGORY*
Advertising

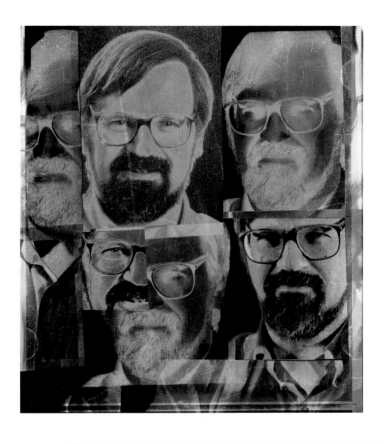

## PORTRAIT #2

*PHOTOGRAPHER*
Daniel Arsnault

*DIGITAL CREATIVE*
Rob Magiera

*CLIENT*
Discovery Magazine

*SOFTWARE*
Adobe Photoshop

*CATEGORY*
Editorial

## NEW AGE ELDERLY

*PHOTOGRAPHER*
Ed Lowe

*DIGITAL CREATIVE*
Philip Howe

*CLIENT*
Kiwanis

*SOFTWARE*
Adobe Photoshop, Fractal
Design's Painter

*CATEGORY*
Editorial

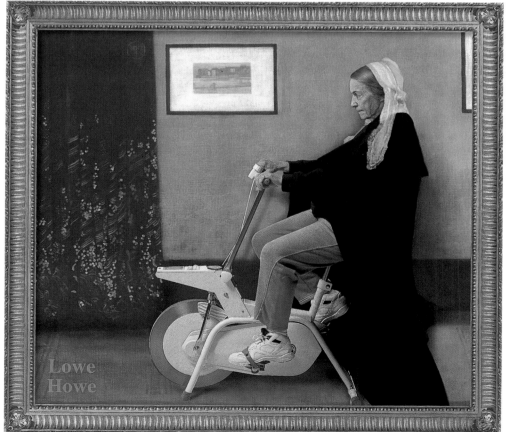

*people*

MEDIA

*media*

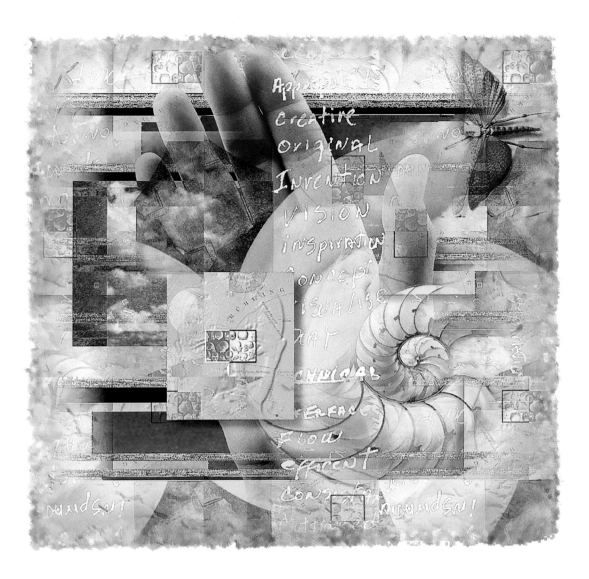

# MARCOLINA DESIGN

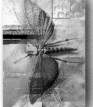

Blending organic hand-crafted qualities with high-tech overtones, this illustration by Marcolina Design, Inc. was used as an interface on their promotional CD-ROM. Conceived to capture the essence and philosophy of the studio, it gracefully balances powerful technology with imaginative beauty. Soft textures and natural objects are translucently overlaid, suggesting growing insight. This is enhanced by the repetition of a window pattern which diffuses through the entire design.

This image was assembled and fashioned in Specular Collage. Working intuitively, the original source imagery was amassed from the studio's CD-ROM collection. Adobe Photoshop was used for masking, color correction, and the integration of text. The final effect incorporates a gentle range of tones and a sense of infinite depth.

With more than fifteen years of experience, Marcolina Design, Inc. is a premiere design and multimedia studio. In this imaginative illustration, they offer a playful example of their design capabilities — while demonstrating part of their versatile design philosophy.

## DIGITAL DEXTERITY

**PHOTOGRAPHER**
Dan Marcolina

**DIGITAL CREATIVES**
Dan Marcolina,
Denise Marcolina,
Dermot MacCormack,
Sean McCabe,
Quinn Richardson,
Mike Lingle,
Matt Peacock

**CLIENT**
Marcolina Design, Inc.

**SOFTWARE**
Adobe Photoshop,
Specular Collage

**CATEGORY**
CD Rom/Interactive

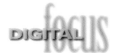

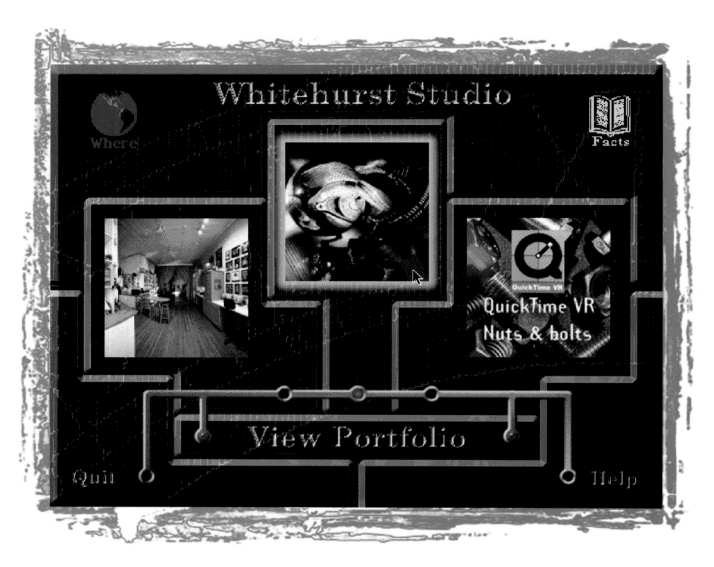

# WILLIAM WHITEHURST

Travel though dimensional space is placed at the viewers finger tips in William Whitehurst's self-promotional CD-ROM. A panoramic photograph of his studio becomes a virtual adventure with the click of the mouse. With total flexibility of motion, it is possible to explore his workspace and even read book titles on the bookshelves. This amazing virtual experience is imaginable through the latest advances in computer technology.

Developed to provide interactive insight into the Whitehurst Studio, the disk offers viewers an opportunity to wander through space and see several different portfolios. It also contains demonstrations of how QuickTimeVR can be used as a conceptual tool. One can navigate through the ideas depicted and select specific information to explore. This new technology also includes an introductory lesson on the interactive interface. The main

**WHITEHURST STUDIO**
*INTERACTIVE CD-ROM*

*PHOTOGRAPHER*
**William Whitehurst**

*DIGITAL CREATIVE*
**William Whitehurst**

*CLIENT*
**Whitehurst Studio**

*SOFTWARE*
**QuicktimeVR,
Apple Media Tool**

*CATEGORY*
**Media**

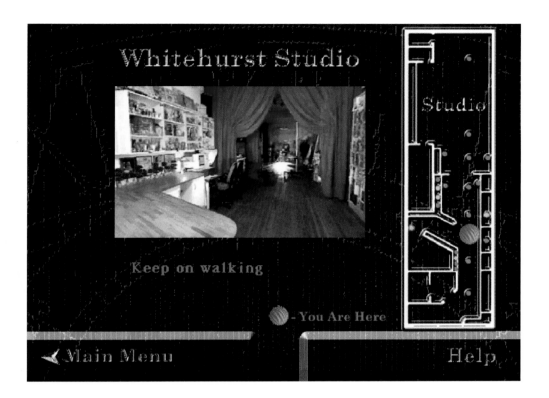

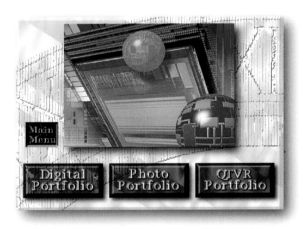

menu invites viewers to choose where to go and what to investigate. Traditional Photography, Digital Imagery and QuickTimeVR tours are all featured in this powerhouse project.

QuickTimeVR converts a photograph into a full motion interaction. Numerous screens and menus were fashioned in Adobe Photoshop. The interface, was generated in Apple Media Tool. Individual images included in the portfolios were created using traditional photography, and both Live Picture and Adobe Photoshop. The overall purpose of the CD's interface was developed to match the style and feel of the dynamic design solutions offered by Whitehurst Studio. The final result is a breathtaking and effective promotional tool.

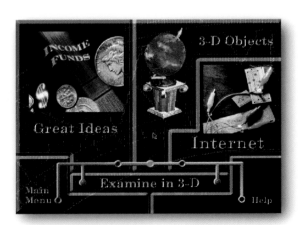

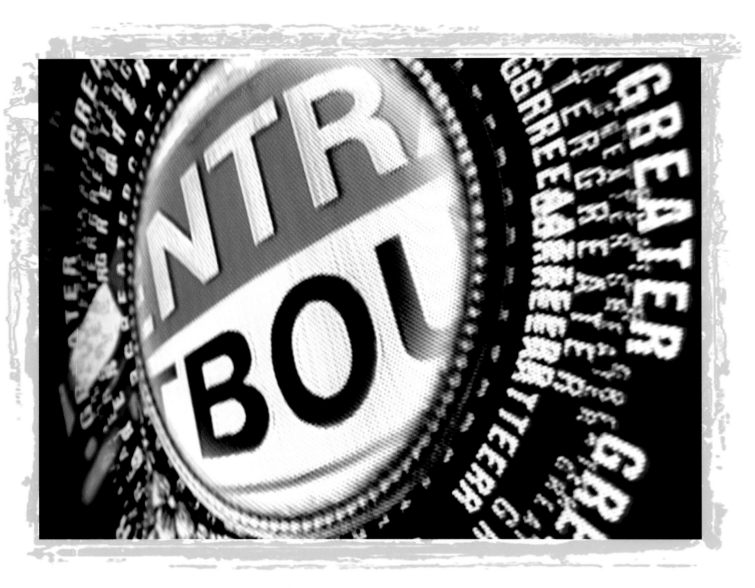

# DALE GRAHAM

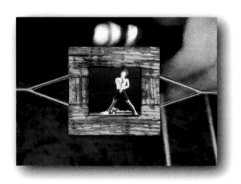

**GREATER BOSTON ARTS**

*DESIGNER*
**Dale Graham**

*PRODUCER*
**Vicky Lemont**

*EDITOR*
**Peter Barstis**

*CLIENT*
**WGBH Boston**

*SOFTWARE*
**Adobe Photoshop,
Adobe Illustrator**

*CATEGORY*
**Broadcast Television**

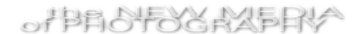

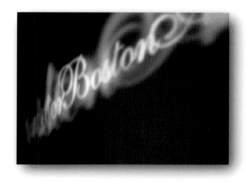

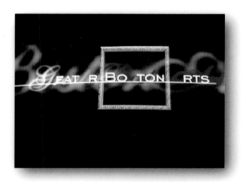

In this imaginative and innovative video for WGBH Boston Public Television both sound and picture get the full creative treatment. Developed to serve as a single promotion and opening sequence for a monthly arts program, Dale Graham and Vicky Lemont of Ouch, employed a cutting-edge approach with a limited budget to the best advantage.

Working with existing footage, they manipulated, and layered their materials. Aimed at uniting the sophistication and the high-energy of Boston, the video juxtaposed classical clips within distorted visual frames. High-speed images of upcoming programming were used to entice viewers, while animated text ran gracefully in sync to an operatic soundtrack.

Ouch pushes the limits of creativity with their wildly adventuresome and intelligent approach. Daring and dynamic their work is both invigorating and inspiring. They bring energy, technical skill and an uncommon vision to meet the toughest design challenges.

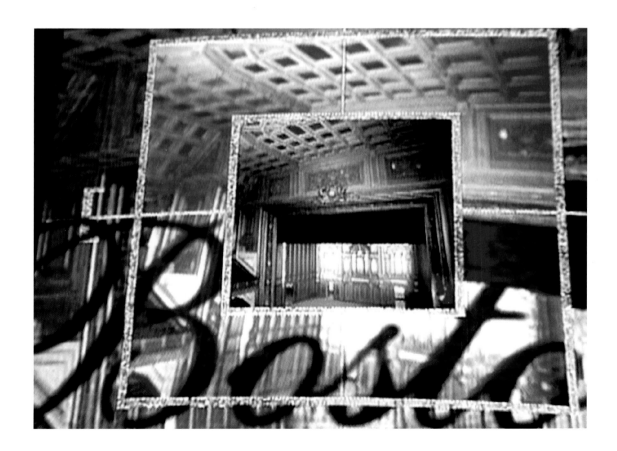

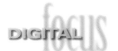

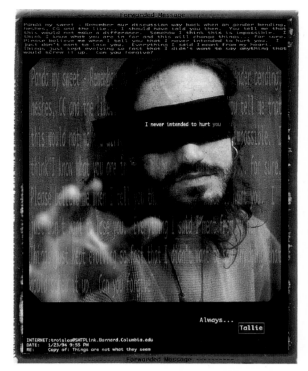

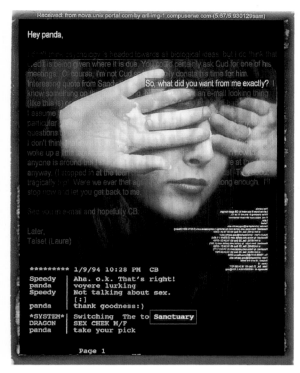

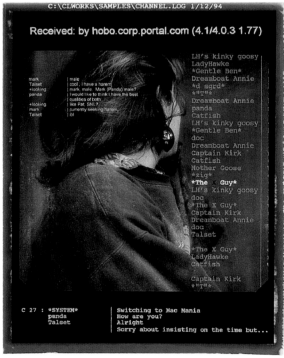

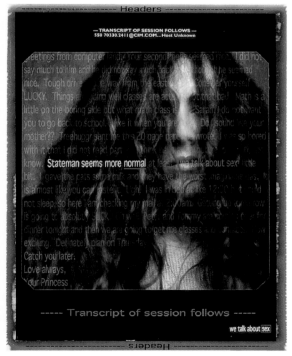

**A.O.L. @**

PHOTOGRAPHER
Mark Katzman

DIGITAL CREATIVE
Mark Katzman

CLIENT
Studio Promotion

SOFTWARE
Live Picture, Fractal Design's
Painter, Adobe Illustrator,
Adobe Photoshop

CATEGORY
Media

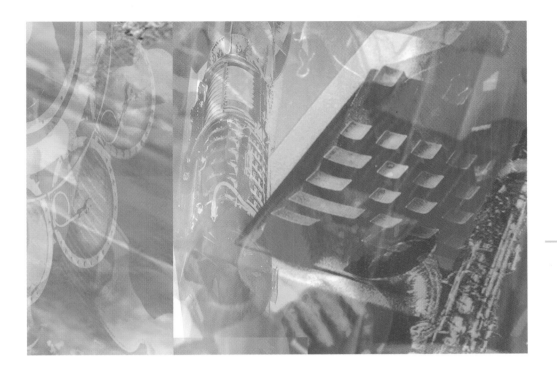

## FRANZ PLAYTIME

*PHOTOGRAPHER*
**Lance Jackson**

*DIGITAL CREATIVE*
**Andrea Sohn**

*CLIENT*
**Franz**

*SOFTWARE*
**Adobe Photoshop**

*CATEGORY*
**Software Packaging**

## CIRCUIT BOARD FACE

*PHOTOGRAPHER*
**Barry Blackman**

*DIGITAL CREATIVE*
**Barry Blackman**

*CLIENT*
**Cyber Kinematic Productions, Ltd.**

*SOFTWARE*
**Barco Creator**

*CATEGORY*
**Web Site**

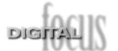

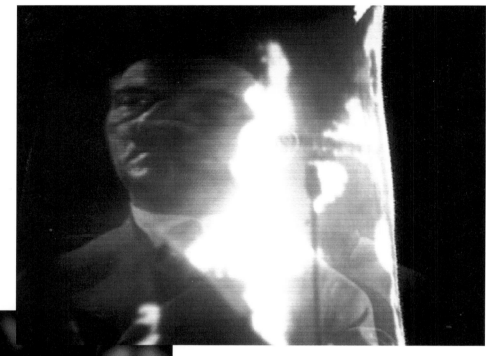

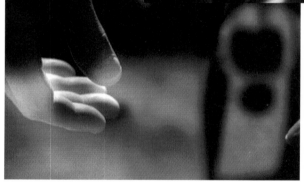

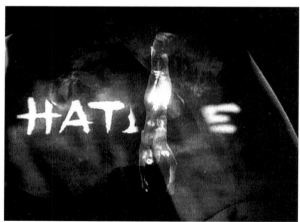

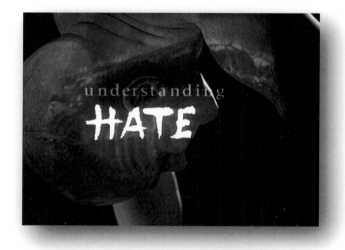

understanding HATE

## UNDERSTANDING HATE

*DESIGNER*
**Dale Graham**

*DIRECTOR/PRODUCER*
**Scott Danielson**

*CLIENT*
**KTCA TV**

*SOFTWARE*
**Macromedia Freehand**

*CATEGORY*
**Broadcast Television**

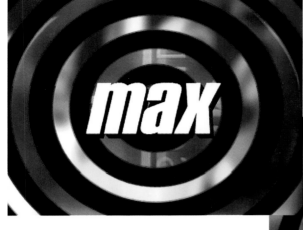

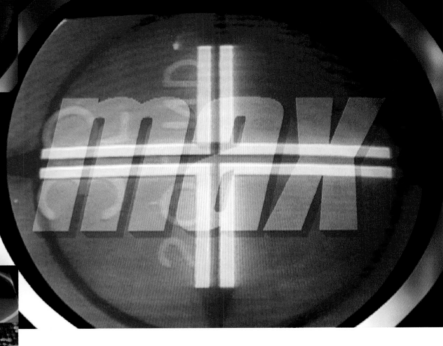

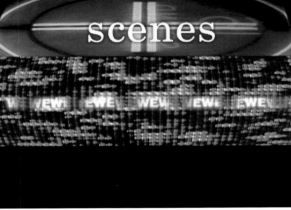

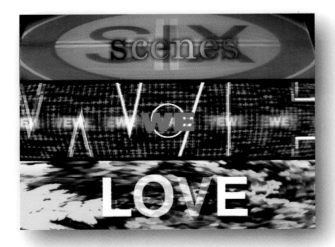

## CINEMAX INTERSTITIAL OPENING GRAPHICS

*DESIGNER*
**Dale Graham**

*PRODUCER*
**Vicky Lemont**

*EDITOR*
**Peter Barstis**

*CLIENT*
**Cinemax**

*SOFTWARE*
**Adobe Photoshop, Adobe Illustrator**

*CATEGORY*
**Cable Television**

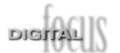

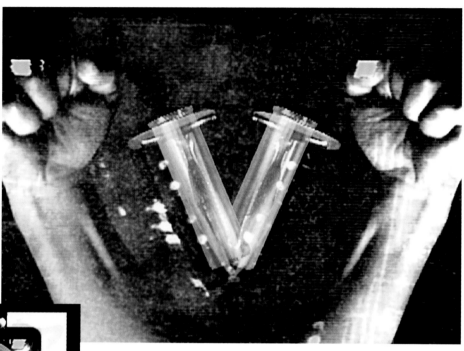

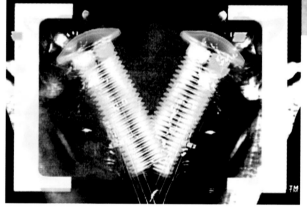

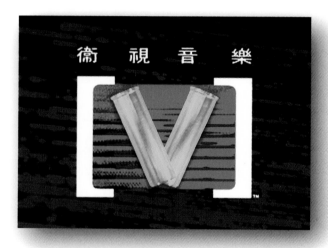

衛 視 音 樂

**CHANNEL V PROMO**

*DESIGNER*
**Dale Graham**

*PRODUCER*
**Hatmaker**

*EDITOR*
**Peter Barstis**

*CLIENT*
**Star TV Asia**

*SOFTWARE*
**Adobe Photoshop,
Adobe Illustrator**

*CATEGORY*
**Cable Television**

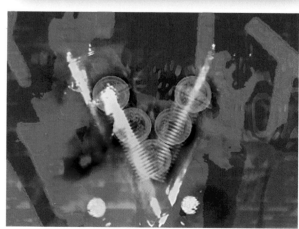

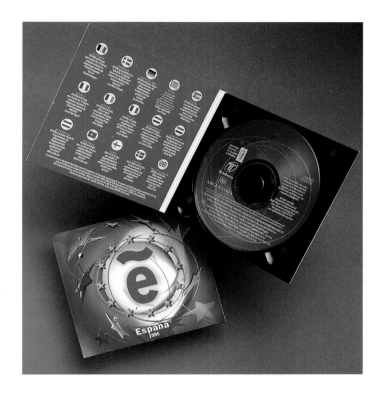

## ẽ

**DIGITAL CREATIVE**
JRDG

**CLIENT**
Government of Spain

**SOFTWARE**
Adobe Illustrator, Adobe Photoshop,
Macromedia Director, Premiere,
Form Z, Electric Image

**CATEGORY**
CD Rom

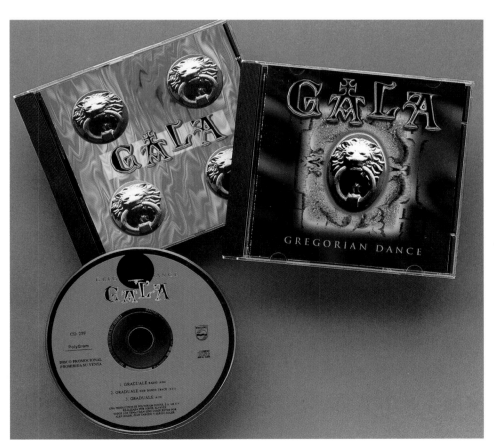

## GALA

**DIGITAL CREATIVE**
JRDG

**CLIENT**
Polygram International

**SOFTWARE**
Adobe Illustrator, Adobe Photoshop, Kay

**CATEGORY**
Music CD Cassette Package

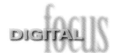

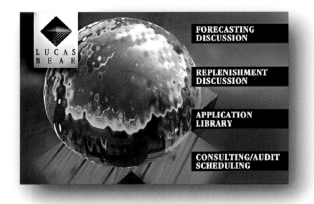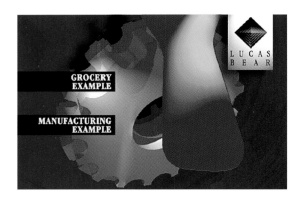

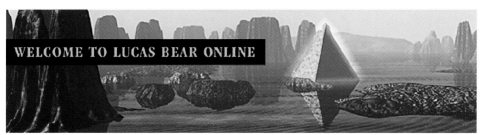

WELCOME TO LUCAS BEAR ONLINE

** THESE ILLUSTRATIONS WERE CREATED BY THE ARTIST WHILE WORKING AT MARCOLINA DESIGN, INC. / TYPE IMPLEMENTATION AND LUCAS BEAR LOGO DESIGN BY DAN MARCOLINA

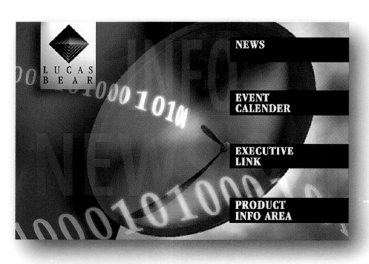

**LUCAS-BEAR ONLINE**

*DIGITAL CREATIVE*
Matthew Peacock**/Anonymous
Productions

*CLIENT*
Lucas-Bear, Inc.

*SOFTWARE*
Adobe Photoshop, Adobe
Illustrator, Infini-D, KPT Bryce

*CATEGORY*
Media

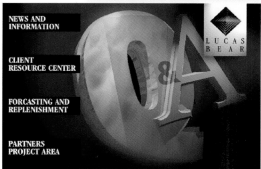

**ODYSSEY SYSTEMS WEBSITE**
(www.iliad.com)

*DIGITAL CREATIVE*
Matthew Peacock/Anonymous
Productions

*CLIENT*
Odyssey Systems Corporation

*SOFTWARE*
Adobe Photoshop, Adobe
Illustrator, Infini-D, Fractal
Design's Painter

*CATEGORY*
Media

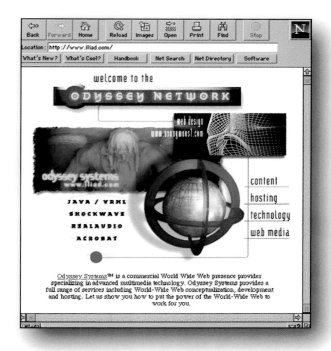

**IKON WEBSITE**
(www.ikon.com)

*DIGITAL CREATIVE*
Matthew Peacock/Anonymous
Productions

*CLIENT*
IKON Office Solutions

*SOFTWARE*
Adobe Photoshop,
Adobe Illustrator,
Fractal's Design Painter

*CATEGORY*
Media

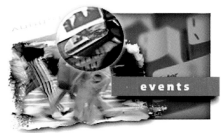

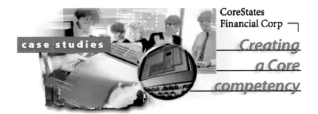

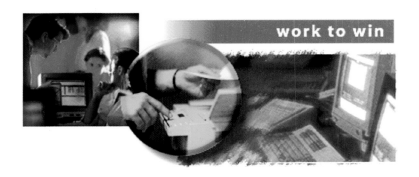

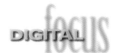

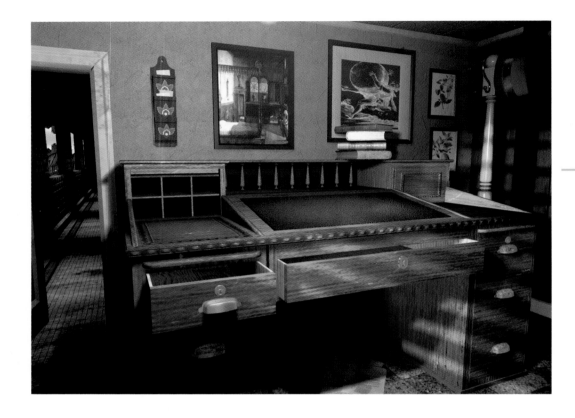

## THE PATENT OFFICE

**PHOTOGRAPHER**
Stock, Henk Dawson

**DIGITAL CREATIVE**
Henk Dawson

**CLIENT**
Microsoft

**SOFTWARE**
Form Z, Electric Image,
Adobe Photoshop

**CATEGORY**
Online

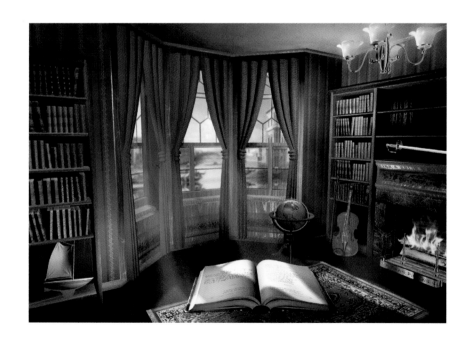

## THE LIBRARY

**PHOTOGRAPHER**
Stock, Henk Dawson

**DIGITAL CREATIVE**
Henk Dawson

**CLIENT**
Microsoft

**SOFTWARE**
Form Z, Electric Image,
Adobe Photoshop

**CATEGORY**
Online

## OBSERVATORY

*PHOTOGRAPHER*
**Stock, Henk Dawson**

*DIGITAL CREATIVE*
**Henk Dawson**

*CLIENT*
**Microsoft**

*SOFTWARE*
**Form Z, Electric Image,
Adobe Photoshop**

*CATEGORY*
**Online**

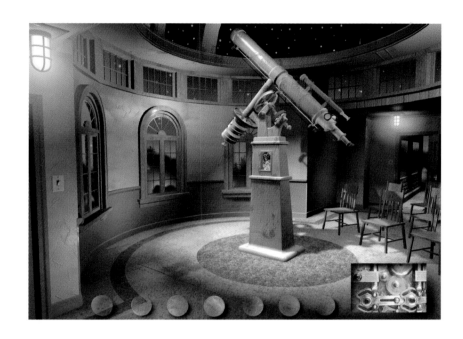

## CONTROL TOWER

*PHOTOGRAPHER*
**Mike Fizer**

*DIGITAL CREATIVE*
**Henk Dawson**

*CLIENT*
**Landor Associates**

*SOFTWARE*
**Form Z, Electric Image,
Adobe Photoshop**

*CATEGORY*
**Advertising**

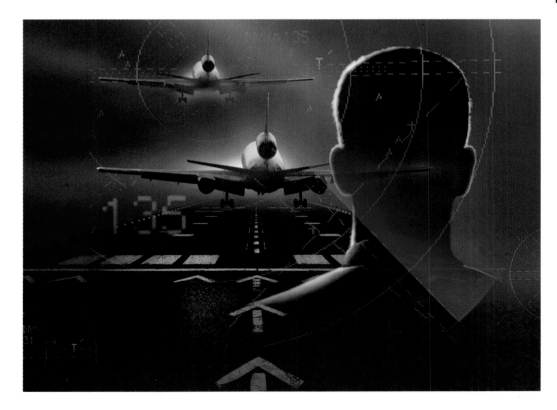

SURREAL

surreal

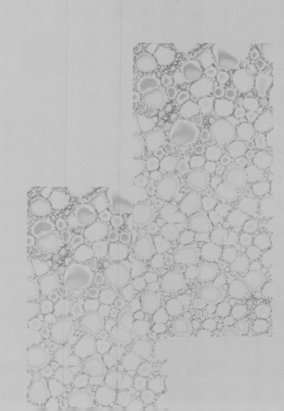

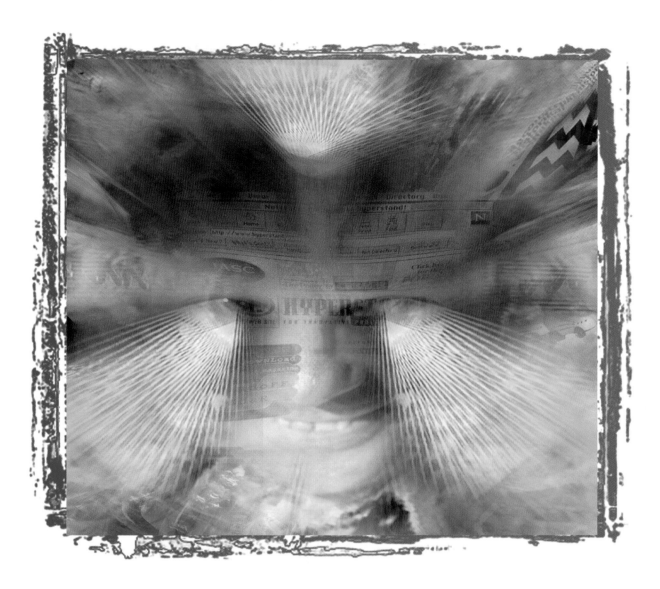

# LANCE JACKSON

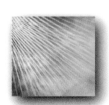

Commissioned as a cover assignment, this kinetic illustration demonstrates the audio and visual capabilities of the Internet. Alluding to wizards and superheros, Jackson has created a parody of happiness and self-enlightenment. Swirling with carnival ride action and color, the smiling figure becomes a wild embodiment of power.

Photographs and still-frames, captured from video, were imported into Adobe Photoshop. Jackson uses a variety of filters and effects to create the richly saturated colors. The kaleidoscopic motion and the artificial sense of atmosphere, add energy to the chaotic excitement of the image.

Jackson is the quintessential digital designer. Grounded in the history of illustration, painting and cult films, he uses the computer with confidence and pushes the limits of both photography and the electronic palette.

**STREAMING FACE**

*PHOTOGRAPHER & VIDEO*
**Lance Jackson**

*DIGITAL CREATIVE*
**Nancy Cutler**

*CLIENT*
**New Media Magazine**

*SOFTWARE*
**Adobe Photoshop**

*CATEGORY*
**Editorial &
Self-Promotion**

SURREAL

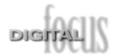

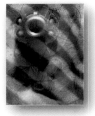

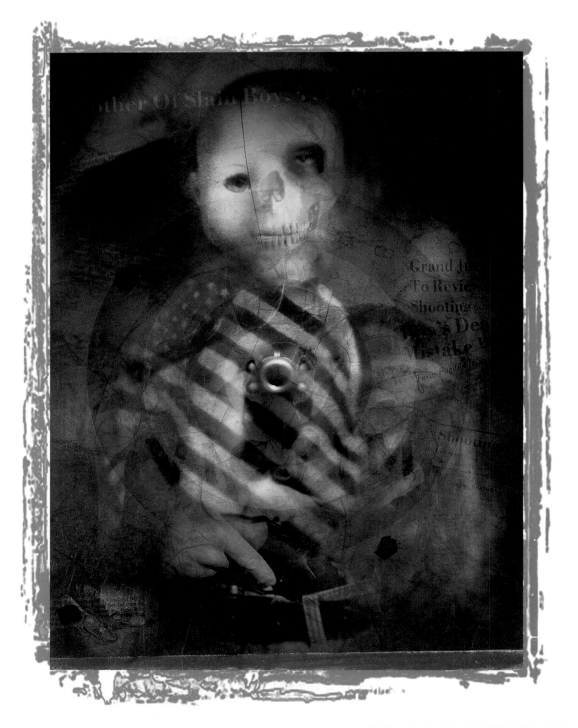

GUNS IN AMERICA

PHOTOGRAPHER
Scott Ferguson

DIGITAL CREATIVE
Scott Ferguson

ART DIRECTOR
Richard Boddy

CLIENT
Discover Magazine

SOFTWARE
Live Picture,
Fractal Design's Painter,
Adobe Illustrator,
Adobe Photoshop

CATEGORY
Editorial

SCOTT
FERGUSON

SURREAL

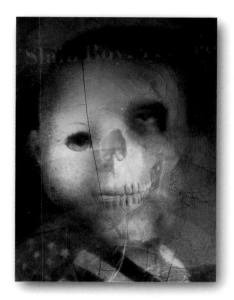

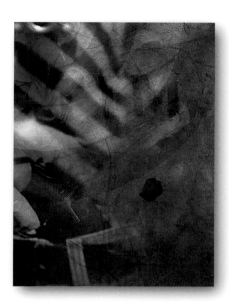

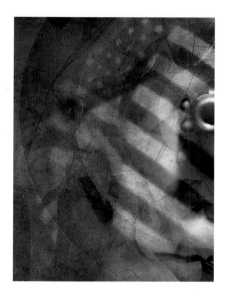

This haunting image of violence in America was created by Scott Ferguson, of Ferguson and Katzman Photography, for *Discover Magazine*. Provided with the storyline for an article on handgun abuse, Ferguson independently conceived and developed this complex, layered illustration. Brutally confrontational and unsettling, the foreboding image evokes a variety of subliminal messages.

Working initially in Live Picture, the primary photographic elements were collated and assembled. Once the basic composition was created, Adobe Photoshop was used for blending, precise channeling, and type treatment. A muted color range was incorporated to enhance both the dangerous uncertainty and the illustrative sense of the work.

Ferguson provides this image with a visual vocabulary as deeply complex and varied as the topic. Initially, the viewer is immediately drawn to the overlapped skull and face of the doll. The reaching hand and the barrel of the gun make a pointedly aggressive statement. The most ominous details remain hidden until the eye becomes acclimated to the darkness; only then do disturbing headlines, prone bodies and violent warnings emerge. This sophisticated approach, to even the most difficult concept, is a signature of Ferguson and Katzman Photography.

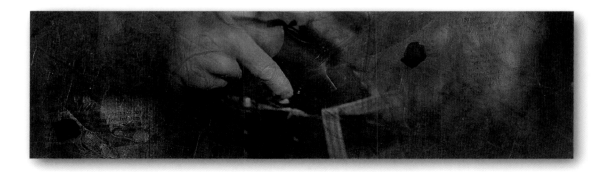

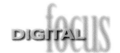

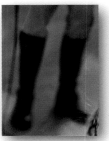

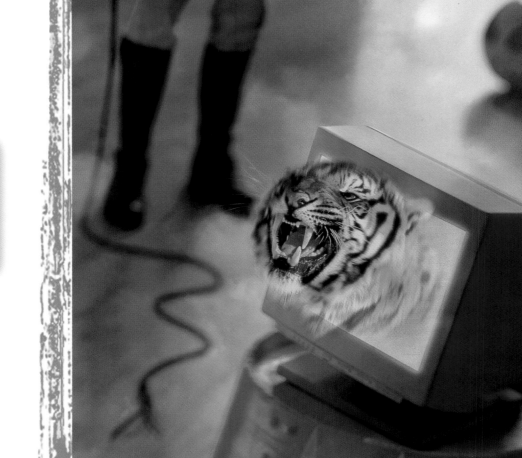

# TOM
# COLLICOTT

This pleasing, mysterious image by Tom Collicott was originally designed to illustrate a *U.S. News and World Report* article entitled "Taming the Internet." Softly focusing on nuance and detail, the piece gently coaxes the viewer to complete its meaning. The tilted frame and intersection of visual elements, hint at danger — yet, the quiet colors and relaxed stance imply a calm readiness to face the task.

The image was assembled in Adobe Photoshop from three separate photographs. Collicott created the base picture of the ringmaster, barrel and computer screen; then, he imported the stock image of the tiger's head. The cloud texture was added to create atmosphere. Filters and color corrections were applied to create the soft focus and enhance the underlying mood of the work.

This beautifully balanced image includes only what is essential to convey its purpose. Typical of Collicott's sensitive style, he uncovers the fundamental concerns in the concepts, and finds visual answers that are both elegant and graceful.

**TIGER TRAINER**

*PHOTOGRAPHER*
**Tom Collicott**
**Tiger:Image Bank Stock**

*DIGITAL CREATIVE*
**Tom Collicott**

*CLIENT*
**US News & World Report**

*SOFTWARE*
**Adobe Photoshop**

*CATEGORY*
**Editorial**

SURREAL

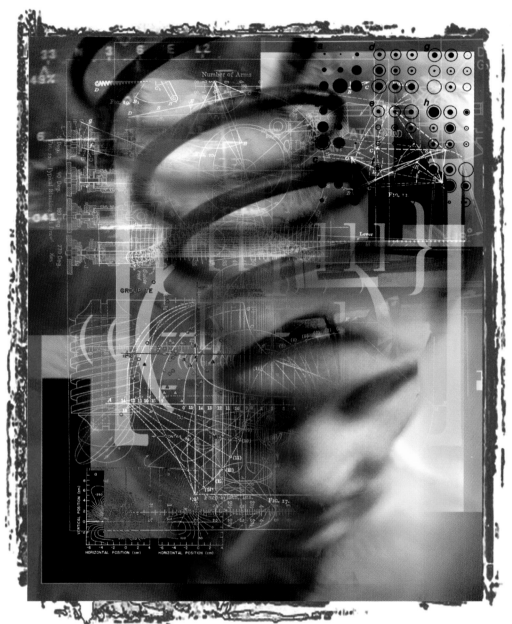

**SPRINGHEAD**

*ILLUSTRATOR*
**Jeff Brice**

*SOFTWARE*
**Adobe Photoshop,
Specular Collage**

*CATEGORY*
**Promotion**

# JEFF BRICE

This self-promotional by Jeff Brice, suggests the process of turning ideas into actions by connecting the industrial with the human. Contemplative and sound, this work uses visual depth and overlapping imagery to explore the association between the informative and cognitive realms of the mind. The central theme of the spring provides a strong graphic impact, demonstrating the powerful energy of thought.

Initially, high resolution scans of photographs and diagrams were generated. To assemble and adjust the layout, low resolution proxies were created in Specular Collage. Working with proxies allowed the design process to flow in real time. Finally, using filters and special effects in Adobe Photoshop, blurring, opacity and color were manipulated.

In this dynamic examination of the creative process, Brice establishes a bridge between form and content. The beauty of the image is balanced by the ideas that it contains. His clear, visual, metaphoric sense allows him to use type, texture, translucence and layering in a complex yet most compelling way.

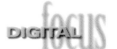

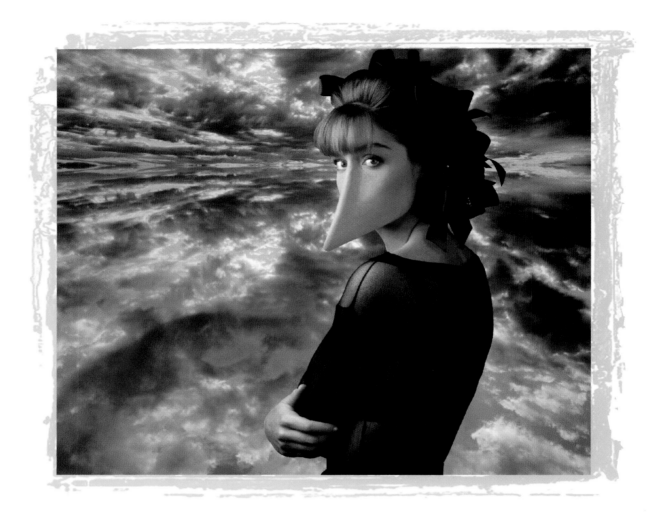

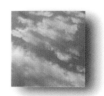

# RICK DUNN

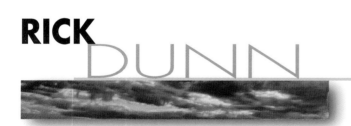

**NOSE JOB**

**PHOTOGRAPHER**
Rick Dunn

**DIGITAL CREATIVE**
Rick Dunn

**CLIENT**
Rick Dunn

**SOFTWARE**
Adobe Photoshop

**CATEGORY**
Promotion

Combining the familiar with the bizarre, Rick Dunn's self-promotion image is firmly planted in the tradition of the surreal. Using the language of the subconscious, what is normally understood becomes radically transformed. In this imaginative world, the viewer's disbelief is at once supported by the photo-realism of the image, yet called into question by the impossibility of the scene.

The photographic elements were first scanned into Adobe Photoshop. Dunn then used scaling, distortion and cloning to achieve the exaggerated facial effect. Visual noise was added to make the cloning closely match the original skin texture. A highly saturated color palette enhanced the mood of the image.

Rick Dunn enjoys fusing uncommon elements in his work. Interested in the line between reality and fiction, he has balanced photo-realism with fantasy to achieve his thought-provoking images. This illustration demonstrates an intuitive creative process using digital manipulation.

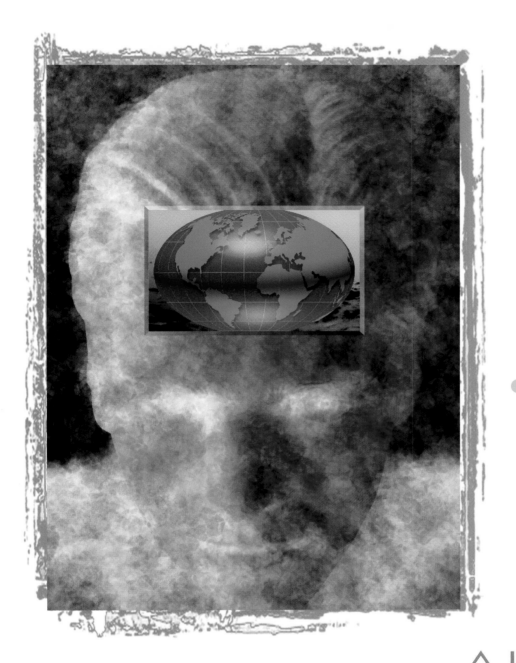

THINKING GLOBALLY

**PHOTOGRAPHER**
Tim Alt

**DIGITAL CREATIVE**
Tim Alt

**SOFTWARE**
Adobe Photoshop, Strata
Studio Pro

**CATEGORY**
Stock

**TIM**
ALT

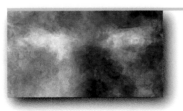

Delving into the realm of dreams, this stock image by Tim Alt, explores the concept of thinking globally. In a unique twist, the man is represented as an element of nature; while the earth is pictured in abstract modern relief. Using the soft colors of space, the human figure blends into a darker surrounding cosmos. Windowed into the mind of the man, a brightly colored world map stands out in sharp contrast.

Filters and color reversing features in Xaos Filters were used to produce the texture and palette of the background figure. The saturated foreground elements were generated in Strata Studio Pro. The image was assembled and further enhanced using Adobe Photoshop.

This thoughtful design solution uses an equated reality to quietly explore and expand on a common phrase. It creates a mood, even as it raises questions. Alt's work often has a powerful high-tech look. In this more painterly example, he shows the diversity and impact of his talent.

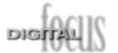

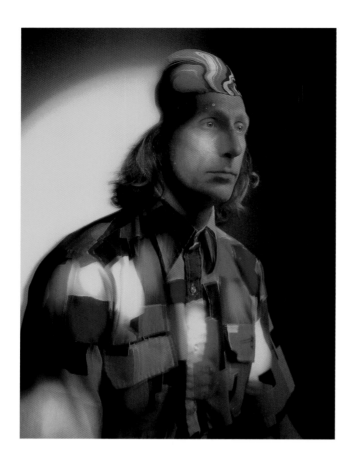

## TODD

*PHOTOGRAPHER*
Stan Musilek

*DIGITAL CREATIVE*
Stan Musilek

*CLIENT*
Stan Musilek

*SOFTWARE*
Live Pictures

*CATEGORY*
Self-Promotion

## DOGBOYS LOST IN THE CITY OF THE FUTURE

*PHOTOGRAPHER*
Ronald Dunlap

*DIGITAL CREATIVE*
Ronald Dunlap

*CLIENT*
Doglight Studios

*SOFTWARE*
Adobe Photoshop

*CATEGORY*
Promotion

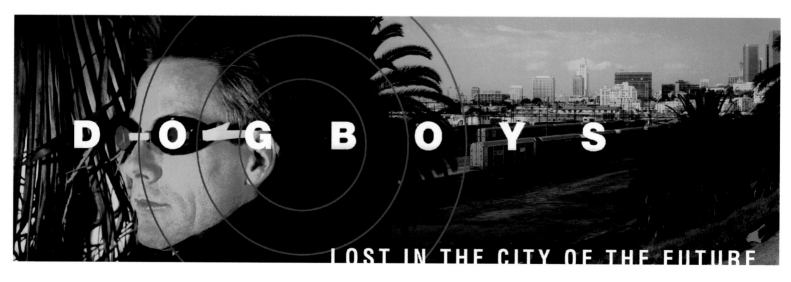

*surreal*

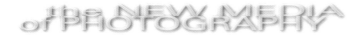

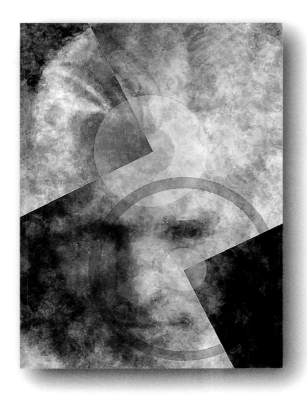

### HEAD WITH BLUE TRIANGLES

*PHOTOGRAPHER*
**Tim Alt**

*DIGITAL CREATIVE*
**Tim Alt**

*SOFTWARE*
**Adobe Photoshop**

*CATEGORY*
**Stock**

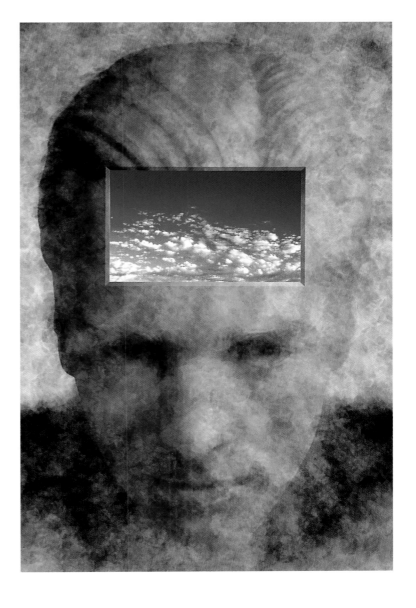

### HEAD WITH CLOUDS

*PHOTOGRAPHER*
**Tim Alt**

*DIGITAL CREATIVE*
**Tim Alt**

*SOFTWARE*
**Adobe Photoshop, Strata Studio Pro**

*CATEGORY*
**Stock**

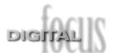

## ACCESS HEAD

*PHOTOGRAPHER & VIDEO*
Lance Jackson

*DIGITAL CREATIVE*
Clay James, Dahlin Smith &
White

*CLIENT*
Sybase

*SOFTWARE*
Adobe Photoshop

*CATEGORY*
Advertising

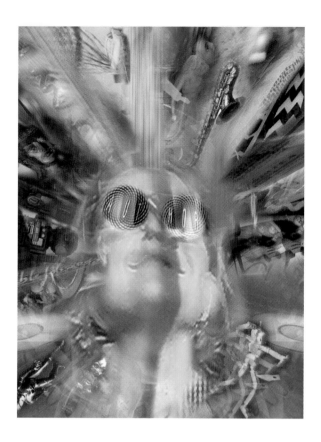

## LINE MAN

*PHOTOGRAPHER*
Rick Dunn

*DIGITAL CREATIVE*
Rick Dunn

*CLIENT*
Rick Dunn

*SOFTWARE*
Adobe Photoshop

*CATEGORY*
Promotion

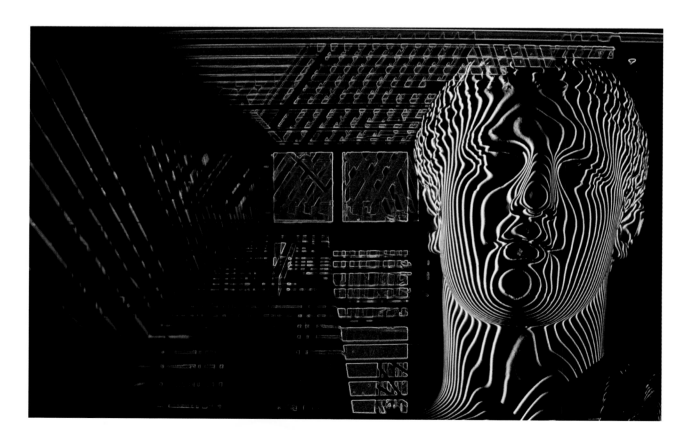

*surreal*

## OVERWIRED

**PHOTOGRAPHER & VIDEO**
Lance Jackson, Craig Lee

**DIGITAL CREATIVE**
Kelly Frankeny

**CLIENT**
San Francisco Examiner

**SOFTWARE**
Adobe Photoshop

**CATEGORY**
Editorial

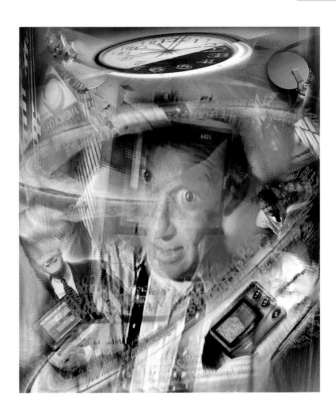

## CEO

**PHOTOGRAPHER & VIDEO**
Susan McMullen, Lance Jackson, Craig Lee

**DIGITAL CREATIVE**
Greg Rattenborg/Bob Coontz Design

**CLIENT**
US West

**SOFTWARE**
Adobe Photoshop

**CATEGORY**
Conference Brochure

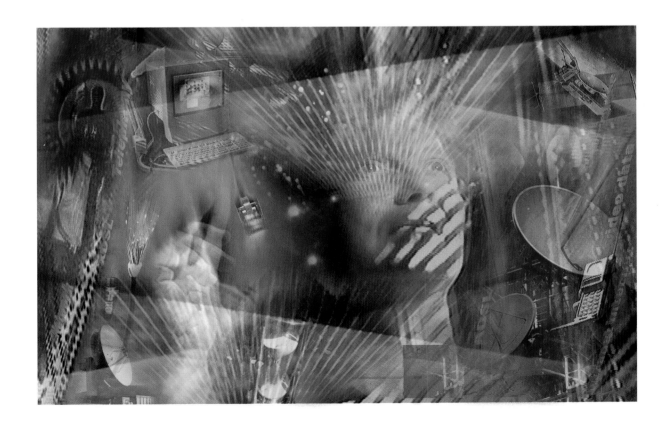

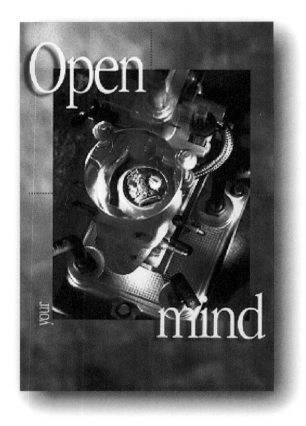

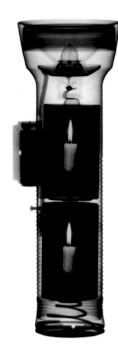

**FLASHLIGHT**

*DIGITAL CREATIVE*
Logan Seale

*CLIENT*
Logan Seale

*SOFTWARE*
Adobe Photoshop

*CATEGORY*
Editorial

**E-BRAIN**

*PHOTOGRAPHER*
Caesar Lima

*DIGITAL CREATIVE*
Caesar Lima

*CLIENT*
Promotion

*SOFTWARE*
Adobe Photoshop

*CATEGORY*
Promotional

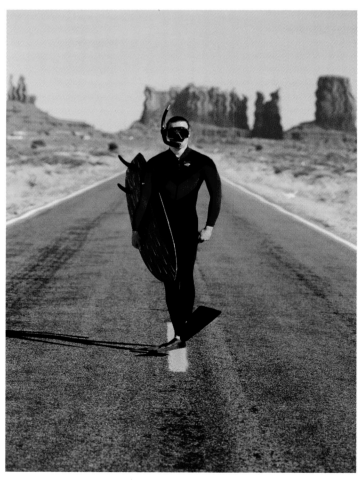

**SCUBA MAN**

*PHOTOGRAPHER*
Nick Koudis

*DIGITAL CREATIVE*
Koudis Nick

*CLIENT*

*SOFTWARE*
Adobe Photoshop

*CATEGORY*
Advertising

SURREAL *surreal*

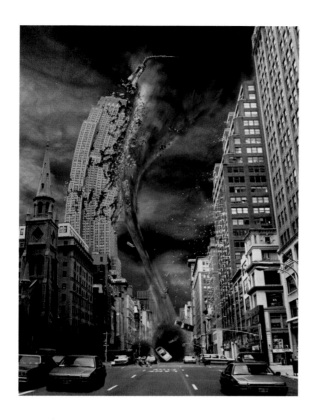

## NEW YORK TWISTER

*PHOTOGRAPHER*
**Barry Blackman**

*DIGITAL CREATIVE*
**Barry Blackman**

*CLIENT*
**Portal Publications**

*SOFTWARE*
**Barco Creator**

*CATEGORY*
**Poster**

## FUTURE HOUSE

*PHOTOGRAPHER*
**Ed Lowe**

*DIGITAL CREATIVE*
**Philip Howe**

*CLIENT*
**Ziff/Davis**

*SOFTWARE*
**Adobe Photoshop,
Fractal Design's Painter**

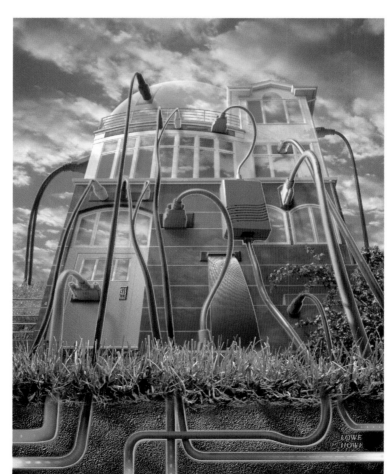

## SKELETON HAND

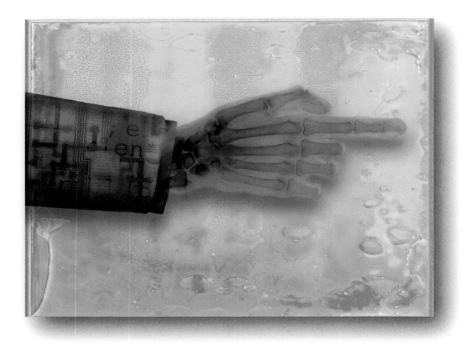

**PHOTOGRAPHER**
Tom Collicott

**DIGITAL CREATIVE**
Tom Collicott

**CLIENT**
Word Perfect Magazine

**SOFTWARE**
Adobe Photoshop

**CATEGORY**
Editorial

## HYPOCRATIC OATH

**PHOTOGRAPHER**
Scott Ferguson

**DIGITAL CREATIVE**
Scott Ferguson

**ART DIRECTOR**
Richard Boddy

**CLIENT**
Discover Magazine

**SOFTWARE**
Live Picture, Fractal Design's
Painter, Adobe Illustrator,
Adobe Photoshop

**CATEGORY**
Editorial

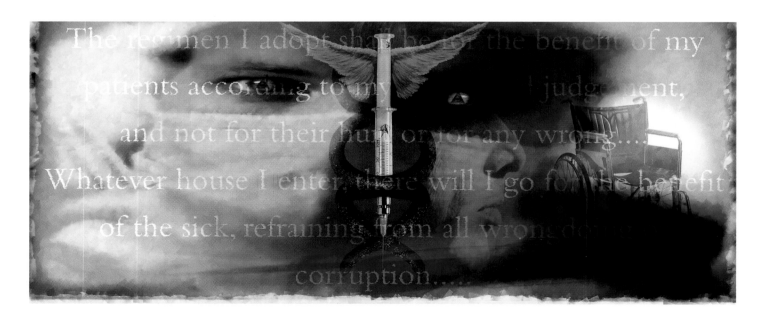

*surreal*

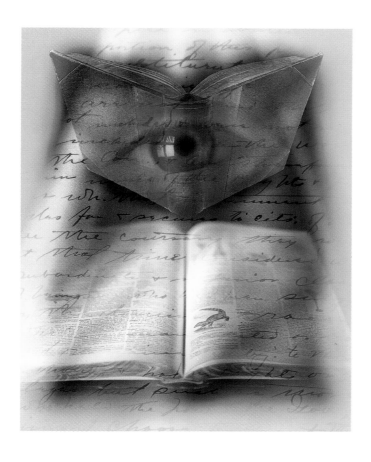

## BOOK/EYE

*PHOTOGRAPHER*
Tom Collicott

*DIGITAL CREATIVE*
Tom Collicott

*CLIENT*
Word Perfect Magazine

*SOFTWARE*
Adobe Photoshop

*CATEGORY*
Editorial

## LOBOTOMY

*PHOTOGRAPHER*
Scott Ferguson

*DIGITAL CREATIVE*
Scott Ferguson

*ART DIRECTOR*
Richard Boddy

*CLIENT*
Discover Magazine

*SOFTWARE*
Live Picture, Fractal Design's Painter,
Adobe Illustrator, Adobe Photoshop

*CATEGORY*
Editorial

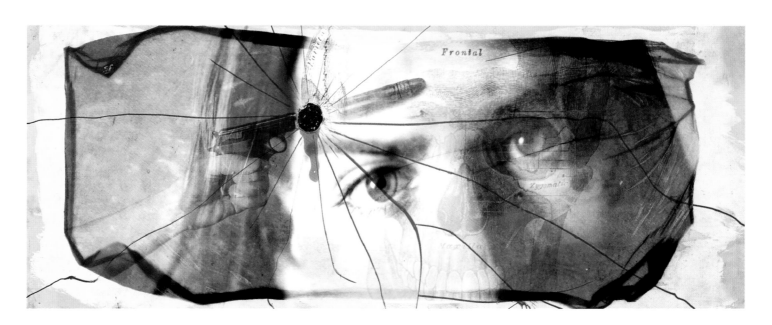

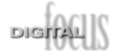

**FIGURE WITH TIMEPIECES**

*PHOTOGRAPHER*
David Chalk

*DIGITAL CREATIVE*
David Chalk

*CLIENT*
William Morrow & Co.

*SOFTWARE*
Barco Creator

*CATEGORY*
Experimental

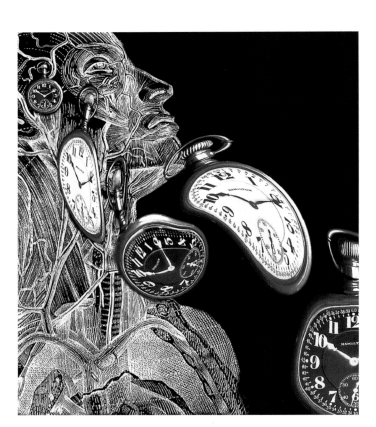

**LOVE HARP**

*PHOTOGRAPHER*
Stock

*DIGITAL CREATIVE*
Eric Berendt

*CLIENT*
Promotion

*SOFTWARE*
Adobe Photoshop

*CATEGORY*
Promotion

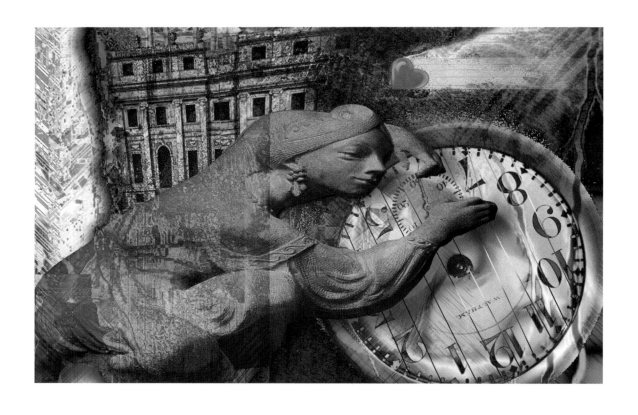

*surreal*

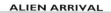

## ALIEN ARRIVAL

*PHOTOGRAPHER*
Stock

*DIGITAL CREATIVE*
Eric Berendt

*CLIENT*
Promotion

*SOFTWARE*
Adobe Photoshop

*CATEGORY*
Promotion

## KLEE TRIUMPHS OVER THE CREATIONISTS

*PHOTOGRAPHER*
Stock

*DIGITAL CREATIVE*
Eric Berendt

*CLIENT*
Promotion

*SOFTWARE*
Adobe Photoshop

*CATEGORY*
Promotion

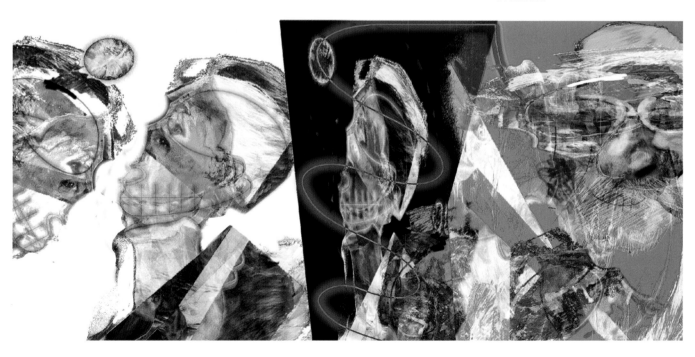

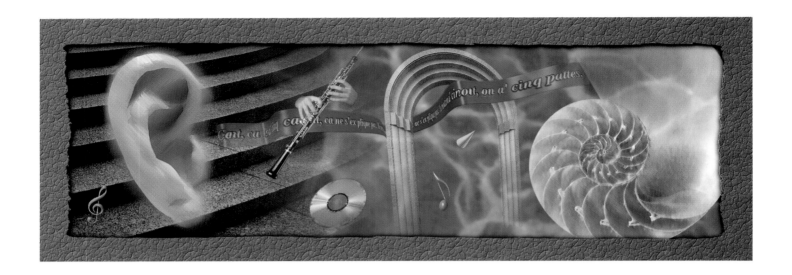

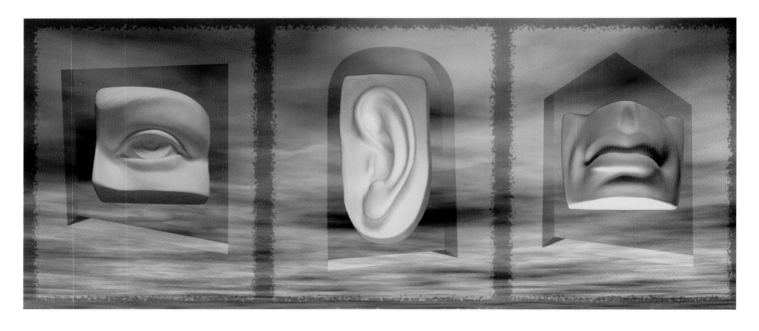

| SOUND | SENSES |
|---|---|
| **PHOTOGRAPHER** | **PHOTOGRAPHER** |
| J.W. Burkey | J.W. Burkey |
| **DIGITAL CREATIVE** | **DIGITAL CREATIVE** |
| J.W. Burkey | J.W. Burkey |
| **CLIENT** | **CLIENT** |
| Stock Image | Stock Image |
| **SOFTWARE** | **SOFTWARE** |
| Live Picture, Adobe Photoshop | Adobe Photoshop |
| **CATEGORY** | **CATEGORY** |
| Stock | Stock |

surreal

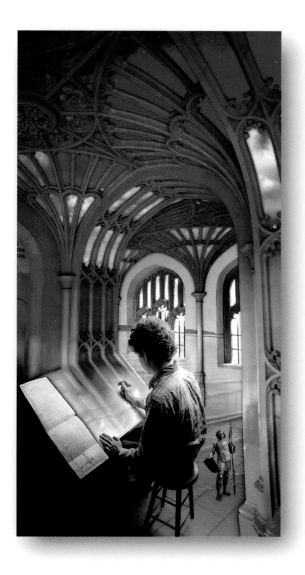

## THE ARCHITECT

*PHOTOGRAPHER*
**Rick Dunn**

*DIGITAL CREATIVE*
**Rick Dunn**

*CLIENT*
**Rick Dunn**

*SOFTWARE*
**Adobe Photoshop, Fractal Design's
Painter**

*CATEGORY*
**Promotion**

## DISCOVERY

*PHOTOGRAPHER*
**Rick Dunn**

*DIGITAL CREATIVE*
**Rick Dunn**

*CLIENT*
**Rick Dunn**

*SOFTWARE*
**Adobe Photoshop, Strada 3D**

*CATEGORY*
**Promotion**

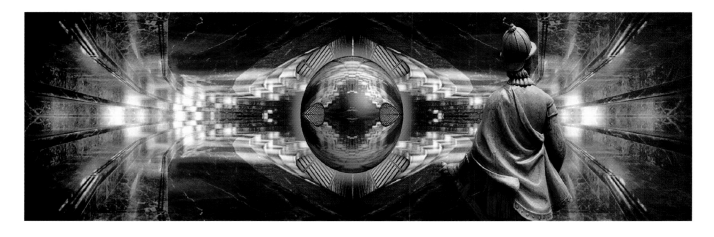

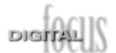

**HEAD GRID**

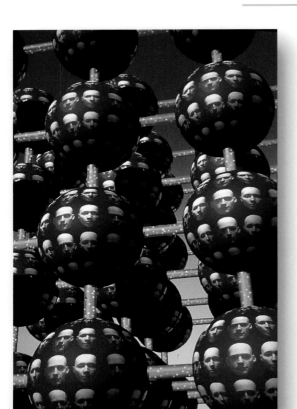

*PHOTOGRAPHER*
Tim Alt

*DIGITAL CREATIVE*
Tim Alt

*SOFTWARE*
Strata 3D, Adobe Photoshop

*CATEGORY*
Stock

**PATHÉ**

*PHOTOGRAPHER*
Stock

*DIGITAL CREATIVE*
Eric Berendt

*CLIENT*
Promotion

*SOFTWARE*
Adobe Photoshop,
Ray Dream Designer

*CATEGORY*
Promotion

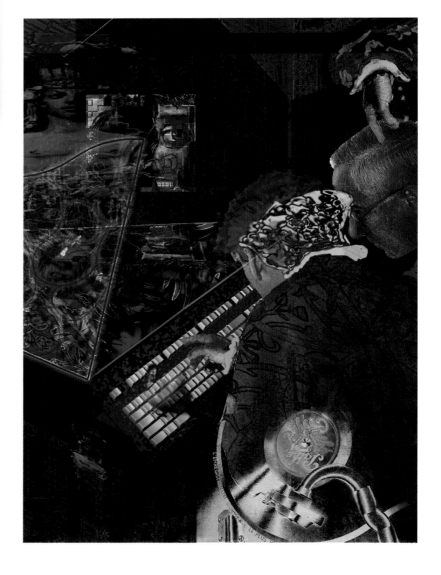

SURREAL

*surreal*

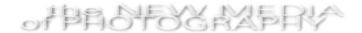

## PASSAGE 4

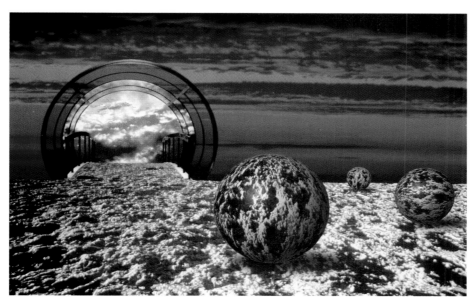

**PHOTOGRAPHER**
Rick Dunn

**DIGITAL CREATIVE**
Rick Dunn

**CLIENT**
Rick Dunn

**SOFTWARE**
Adobe Photoshop, Strada 3D

**CATEGORY**
Promotion

## FLAME HAND; NOUMENA LOGO

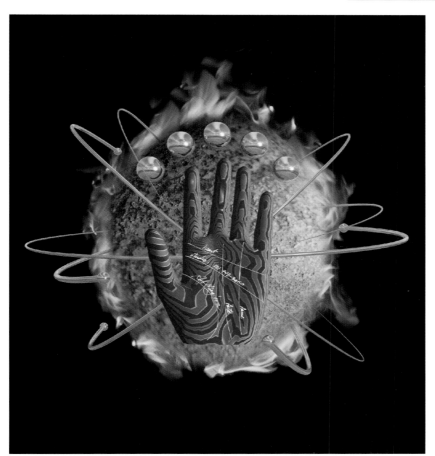

**DIGITAL CREATIVE**
Rob Magiera

**CLIENT**
Personal, Company Logo

**SOFTWARE**
Adobe Photoshop, Alias Sketch!

**CATEGORY**
Self Promotion

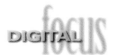

## SUICIDE

**PHOTOGRAPHER**
Scott Ferguson

**DIGITAL CREATIVE**
Scott Ferguson

**ART DIRECTOR**
Richard Boddy

**CLIENT**
Discover Magazine

**SOFTWARE**
Live Picture, Fractal Design's Painter,
Adobe Illustrator, Adobe Photoshop

**CATEGORY**
Editorial

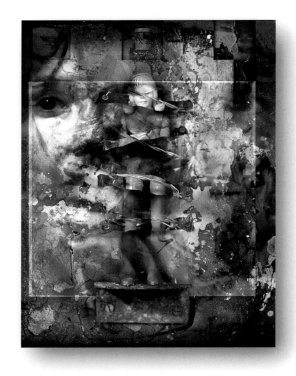

## BRAIN BOY

**PHOTOGRAPHER**
Erik Ostling

**DIGITAL CREATIVE**
Rob Magiera

**CLIENT**
Novell

**SOFTWARE**
Adobe Photoshop,
Alias Sketch!

**CATEGORY**
Advertising

*surreal*

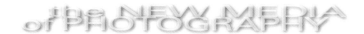

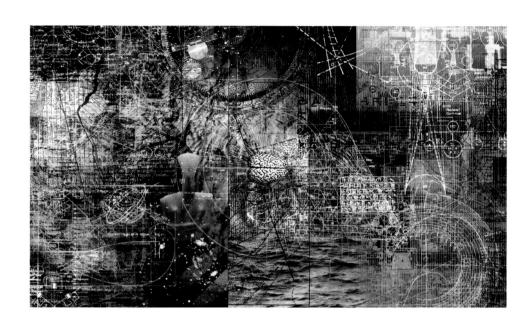

## MNEMONIC

*ILLUSTRATOR*
**Jeff Brice**

*ART DIRECTOR*
**John Plunkett**

*CLIENT*
**Wired Magazine**

*SOFTWARE*
**Adobe Photoshop**

*CATEGORY*
**Editorial**

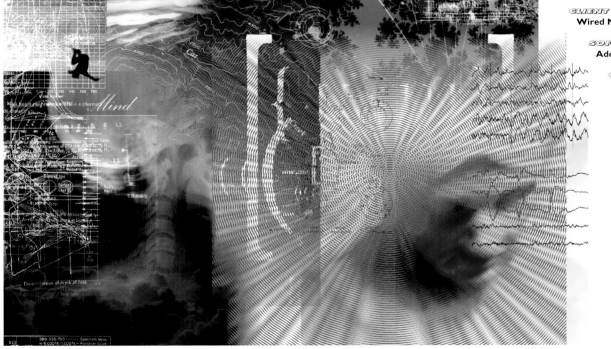

## MNEMONIC

*ILLUSTRATOR*
**Jeff Brice**

*ART DIRECTOR*
**John Plunkett**

*CLIENT*
**Wired Magazine**

*SOFTWARE*
**Adobe Photoshop**

*CATEGORY*
**Editorial**

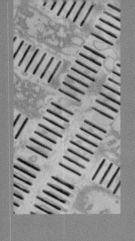

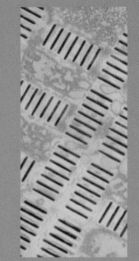

*editorial* EDITORIAL

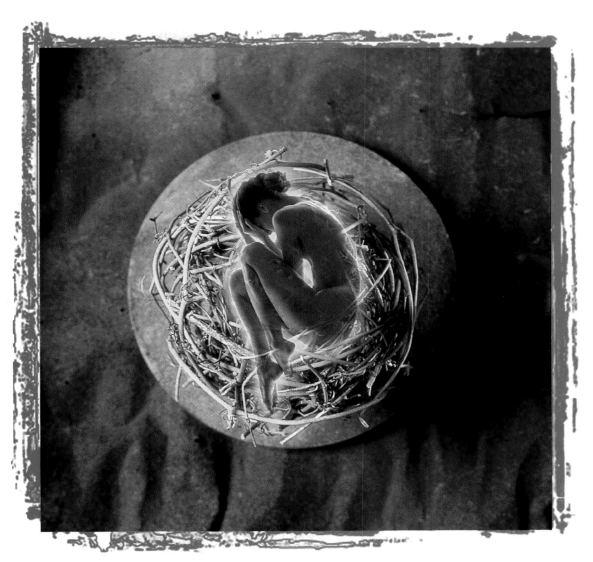

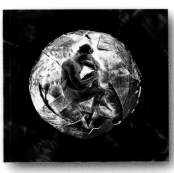

**MALE AND FEMALE COCOON**

*PHOTOGRAPHERS*
**Sharon White/Bob Packert**

*DIGITAL CREATIVES*
**Sharon White/Bob Packert**

*CLIENT*
**MIT Technology Review**

*SOFTWARE*
**Adobe Photoshop, Live Picture**

*CATEGORY*
**Editorial**

# WHITE/
# PACKERT

These emotional images were created for *MIT Technology Review* to illustrate the natural immunity of some people who have been minimally exposed to the AIDS virus. Within the design solution, White/Packert captures both human vulnerability and the concept of protective environments. A male and female figure, shown in fragile posture, are placed in the safety of a nest and a secure metal ball.

The various photographic elements of the images were assembled and layered in Adobe Photoshop using masking and filters to create the dramatic effect. The vivid colors were achieved in Live Picture to enhance the tension and sense of contrast between danger and security.

White/Packert's thoughtful approach conveys the critical relationship between science and the human experience. The rich visual language elaborates the complexity and deep concern of a difficult and griping subject. The strength of this work lies in their ability to identify and develop strong elements and to effectively combine and enhance them.

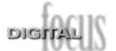

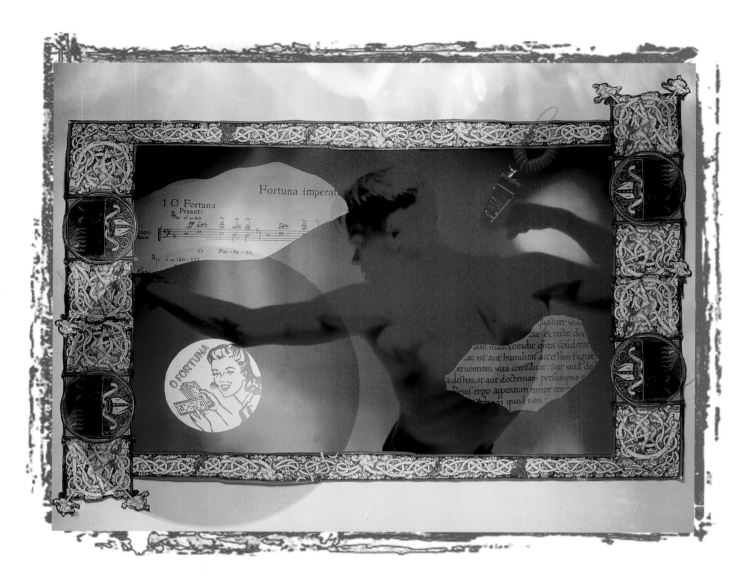

# KEN
# DAVIES

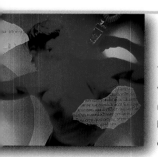

This intriguing tableau, which explores the historical roots of a modern dance record, was created to illustrate a feature article for *Toronto Life Magazine*. It combines elements representing the album called *Oh Fortuna* (the classical work upon which it was based) and the medieval poem that inspired the music. Anchoring these details is the central image of Fortuna, the ancient Roman goddess of good fortune.

Original photographs of the figure and the album were imported into Adobe Photoshop. Scans of torn pieces of sheet music and a section of the ancient poem were positioned around the torso. The elements were then assembled as a collage using varied degrees of opacity and a concentrated, monochromatic set of color values.

An ornate border of the image confines the tension of the figure and makes a connection between past and present. The record overlaps the border and begins to escape the boundaries of historical time. Ken Davies' work is both powerful and intense. This stylized example is typical of his effective visual approach.

## OH FORTUNA

**PHOTOGRAPHER**
**Ken Davies**

**DIGITAL CREATIVE**
**Ken Davies**

**CLIENT**
**Toronto Life Magazine**

**SOFTWARE**
**Adobe Photoshop**

**CATEGORY**
Editorial

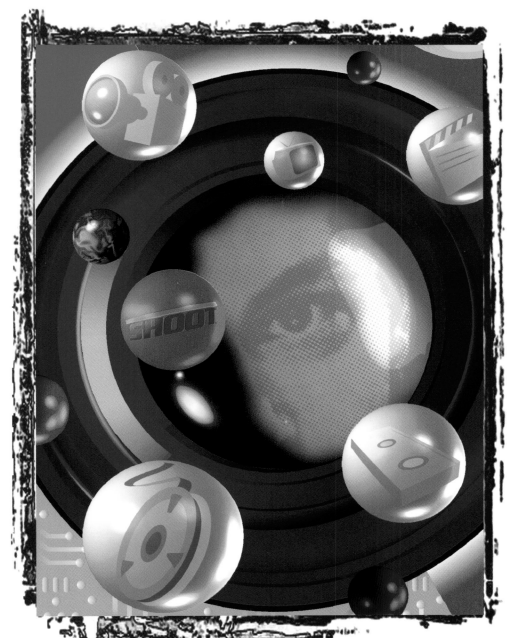

# JAVIER ROMERO

Designed for *Shoot Magazine's* media kit folder cover, this image dynamically conveys the attitude of the publisher. The eye, peering through the lens, captures and records the moving spheres of media. The colorful intersection of components give the design a contemporary, high energy feeling.

The photographic elements were imported into Adobe Photoshop. A high contrast filter was applied to the face to give it a more graphic feel and the colorful spheres were generated. The Shoot logo was imported into Adobe Illustrator and warped to conform to a spherical shape. Movie camera and other media icons were also created in Illustrator. The composition was assembled in Photoshop. Light reflections and the vividly colorful palette were added, creating a sense of depth and action.

For over a decade, Javier Romero Design Group has been helping companies involved in the creative process develop unique and compelling messages for advertising, publishing and media. With studios in New York and Madrid, they bridge the gap between creativity and technology through understanding, experience and innovative thinking.

**SHOOT MAGAZINE**

*DIGITAL CREATIVE*
**JRDG**

*CLIENT*
**Shoot Magazine**

*SOFTWARE*
**Adobe Illustrator,
Adobe Photoshop**

*CATEGORY*
**Media Kit**

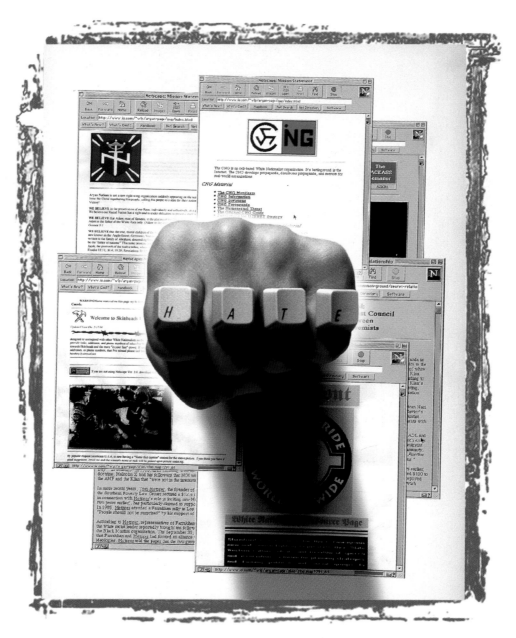

# MIRKO ILIĆ

CYBERHATE

PHOTOGRAPHERS
**Maria Vullo, Tabanitha T. McDaniel**

DIGITAL CREATIVE
**Mirko Ilić**

CLIENT
**Emerge Magazine**

SOFTWARE
**Adobe Photoshop**

CATEGORY
**Editorial**

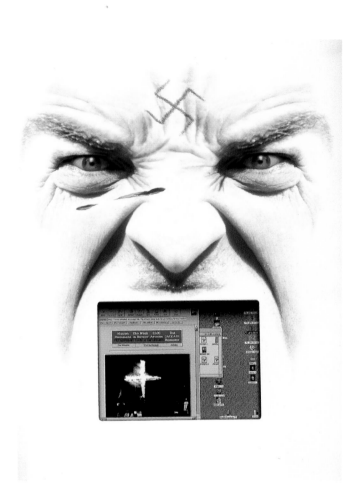

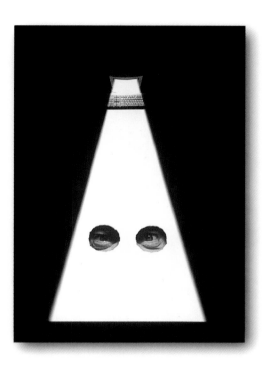

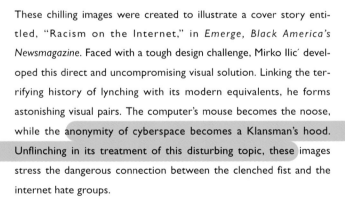

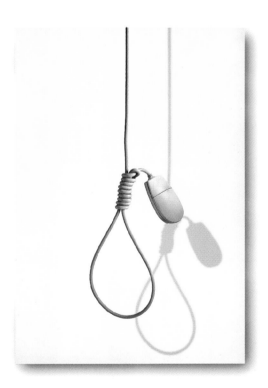

These chilling images were created to illustrate a cover story entitled, "Racism on the Internet," in *Emerge, Black America's
Newsmagazine.* Faced with a tough design challenge, Mirko Ilic´ developed this direct and uncompromising visual solution. Linking the ter-
rifying history of lynching with its modern equivalents, he forms
astonishing visual pairs. The computer's mouse becomes the noose,
while the anonymity of cyberspace becomes a Klansman's hood.
Unflinching in its treatment of this disturbing topic, these images
stress the dangerous connection between the clenched fist and the
internet hate groups.

Working in Adobe Photoshop, objects and graphic elements are
linked with precise control, resulting in a clear, high-impact message.
Shadows, contrast, and exaggerated highlights all add emphasis to
the work. Actual hate group web pages form a visual and factual
background that accentuates the sinister reality of the theme. Ilic´'s
powerful design solutions profoundly impact on the consciousness of
the reader. His work unmasks the truth with convincing portraits of
human circumstance.

127

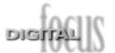

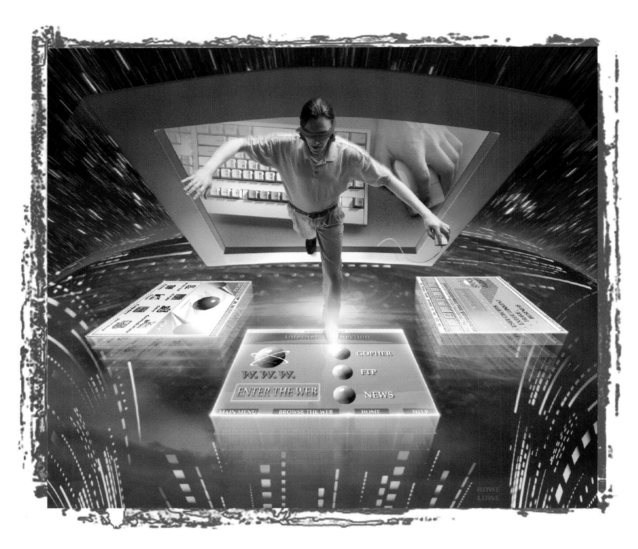

# PHIL
# HOWE

**NET WALK**

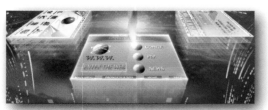

Asked to show the precarious moment when a person first enters the Internet, Phil Howe created this energetic and amusing image. He juxtaposed the fast-paced excitement of stepping into cyberspace, with the tentative balance of blind uncertainty. The design is linked to reality by the hand controlling the mouse. The arms of the figure are reaching for stability, as zips and dashes of data race through net space.

Howe developed a pencil layout and worked with photographer Ed Lowe to create a set of well-matched photographic images. The components were scanned and assembled in Adobe Photoshop. To create the playful sense of tension between reality and illusion, the image was carefully layered, painted, distorted and enhanced. The final result is a concise, easily interpreted illustration.

With more than twenty years of experience as an illustrator and a strong photo-retouching background, he integrates his work with a wide variety of digital manipulation techniques. Howe's clear and creative visual solutions demonstrate his enjoyment in meeting the design needs of the client.

*PHOTOGRAPHER*
**Ed Lowe**

*DIGITAL CREATIVE*
**Philip Howe**

*CLIENT*
**Ziff/Davis Publishing**

*SOFTWARE*
**Adobe Photoshop**

*CATEGORY*
**Editorial**

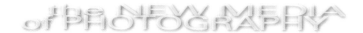

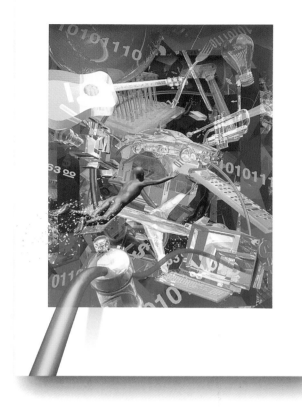

## WELCOME TO CYBERSPACE

*DIGITAL CREATIVES*
Mirko Ilic', Alex Arce

*CLIENT*
Time Magazine

*SOFTWARE*
Soft Image, Adobe Photoshop

*CATEGORY*
Editorial

## CUTTING THE CORD

*PHOTOGRAPHER*
Mike Fizer

*DIGITAL CREATIVE*
Henk Dawson

*CLIENT*
Home Mechanix

*SOFTWARE*
Studio Pro, Adobe Photoshop

*CATEGORY*
Editorial

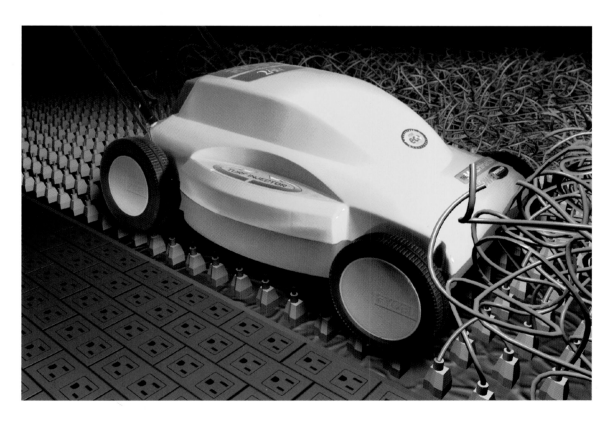

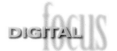

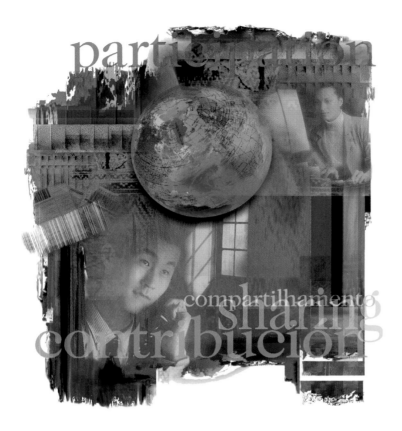

## PARTICIPATION

*PHOTOGRAPHER*
Bob Schlowsky, Stock Images

*DIGITAL CREATIVE*
Lois Schlowsky

*CLIENT*
Moore Business Forms

*SOFTWARE*
QFX, Adobe Photoshop

*CATEGORY*
Magazine Cover

## 4 MOUSE CONTROLS WITH GLOBE IMAGE

*PHOTOGRAPHER*
Ken Davies

*DIGITAL CREATIVE*
Ken Davies

*CLIENT*
Family PC Magazine

*SOFTWARE*
Adobe Photoshop

*CATEGORY*
Editorial

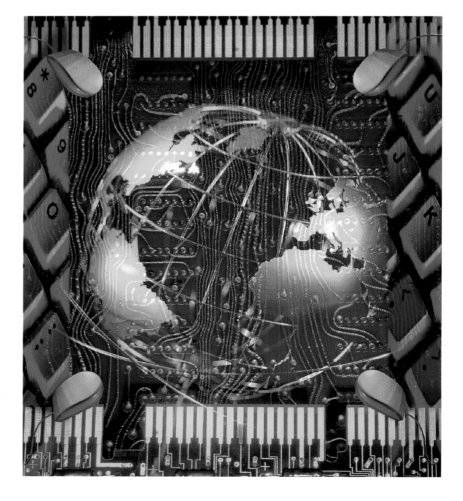

*editorial* EDITORIAL

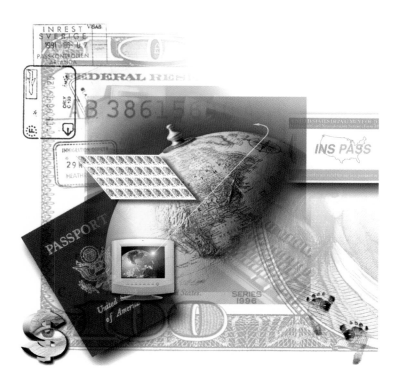

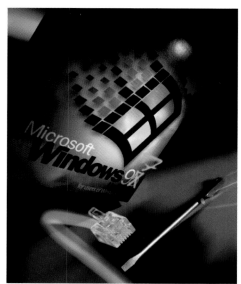

**WINDOWS '97**

*PHOTOGRAPHER*
Logan Seale

*DIGITAL CREATIVE*
Logan Seale

*ART DIRECTOR*
Doug Adams

*CLIENT*
Windows Magazine

*SOFTWARE*
Adobe Photoshop

*CATEGORY*
Editorial

**INTERNAL FEATURE**

*PHOTOGRAPHER*
Bill Milne

*DIGITAL CREATIVE*
Bill Milne

*CLIENT*
Lan Times Magazine

*SOFTWARE*
Adobe Photoshop, Adobe Illustrator

*CATEGORY*
Editorial

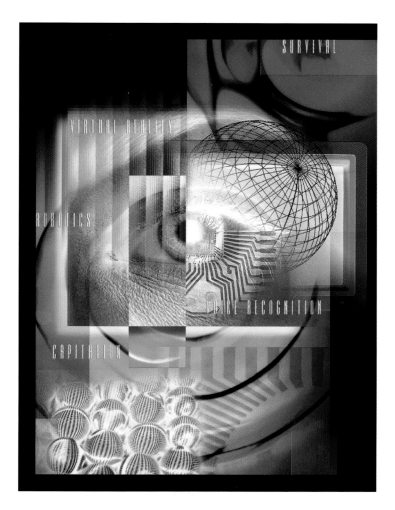

**THE FUTURE OF OPHTHALMOLOGY**

*PHOTOGRAPHER*
Dan Marcolina

*DIGITAL CREATIVE*
Dan Marcolina, Stock

*CLIENT*
Chilton Publishing

*SOFTWARE*
Adobe Photoshop, Specular Collage

*CATEGORY*
Editorial/Medical

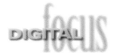

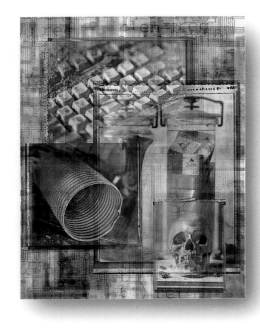

**KEYBOARD/SKULL/PIPE**

*PHOTOGRAPHER*
**Tom Collicott**

*DIGITAL CREATIVE*
**Tom Collicott**

*CLIENT*
**Internet Underground Magazine**

*SOFTWARE*
**Adobe Photoshop**

*CATEGORY*
**Editorial**

**W.W.W.**

*DIGITAL CREATIVE*
**Eric Yang**

*CLIENT*
**Computer Shopper Magazine**

*SOFTWARE*
**Adobe Photoshop**

*CATEGORY*
**Editorial**

**JEEP**

*DIGITAL CREATIVE*
**Eric Yang**

*CLIENT*
**Popular Science Magazine**

*SOFTWARE*
**Adobe Photoshop**

*CATEGORY*
**Editorial**

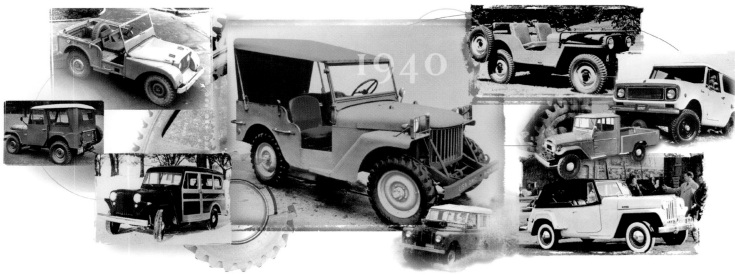

*editorial* EDITORIAL

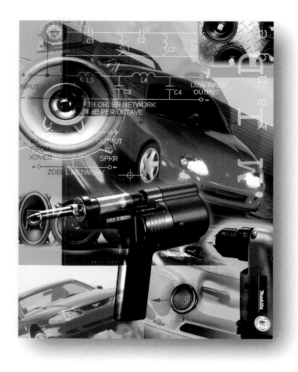

**SPEAKER INSTALLATION**

*DIGITAL CREATIVE*
Eric Yang

*CLIENT*
Car Stereo Review Magazine

*SOFTWARE*
Adobe Photoshop

*CATEGORY*
Editorial

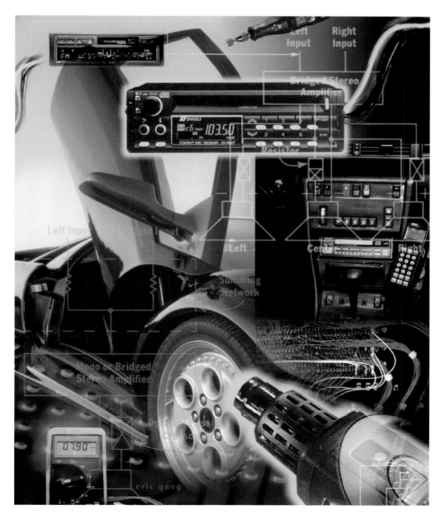

**CD INSTALLATION**

*DIGITAL CREATIVE*
Eric Yang

*CLIENT*
Car Stereo Review Magazine

*SOFTWARE*
Adobe Photoshop

*CATEGORY*
Editorial

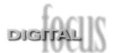

## CAN JUSTICE BE DONE?

*PHOTOGRAPHER*
Mirko Ilić, Stock Photography

*DIGITAL CREATIVE*
Mirko Ilić

*CLIENT*
World Press Review

*SOFTWARE*
Adobe Photoshop

*CATEGORY*
Editorial

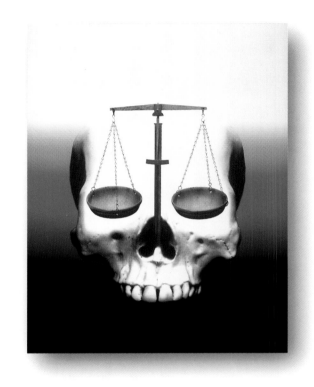

## THE FIRST INTERACTIVE MUSEUM

*PHOTOGRAPHER*
Mirko Ilić,
Stock Photography

*DIGITAL CREATIVE*
Mirko Ilić

*CLIENT*
Swing Magazine

*SOFTWARE*
Adobe Photoshop

*CATEGORY*
Editorial

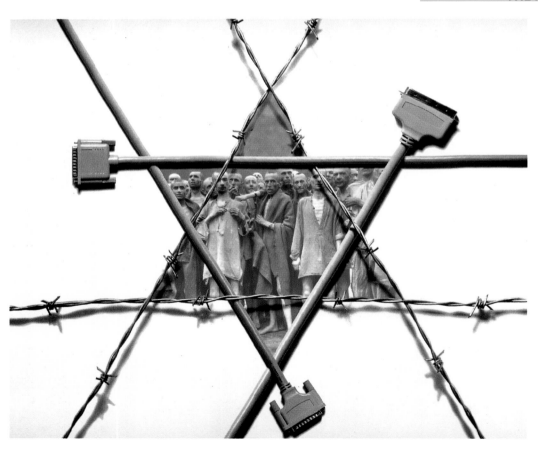

*editorial*

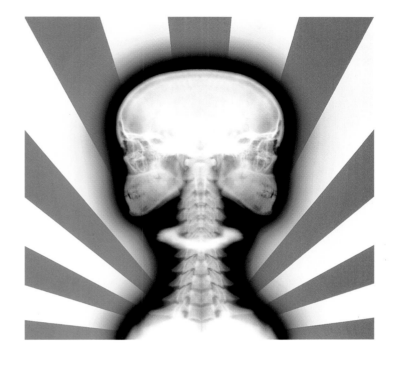

### HIROSHIMA LEGACY

**DIGITAL CREATIVE**
Mirko Ilić

**CLIENT**
New York Times Book Review

**SOFTWARE**
Adobe Photoshop,
Adobe Illustrator

**CATEGORY**
Editorial

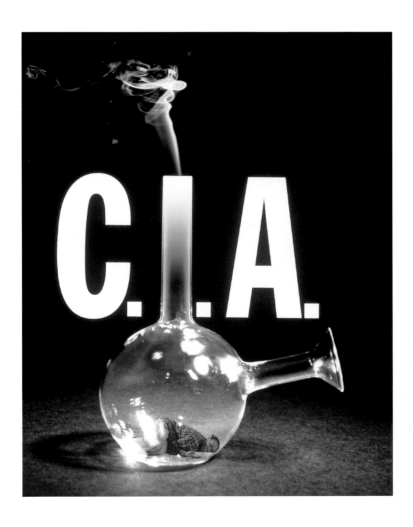

### C.I.A.

**PHOTOGRAPHER**
Maria Vullo

**DIGITAL CREATIVE**
Mirko Ilić

**CLIENT**
Emerge Magazine

**SOFTWARE**
Adobe Photoshop, Adobe Illustrator

**CATEGORY**
Editorial

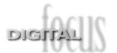

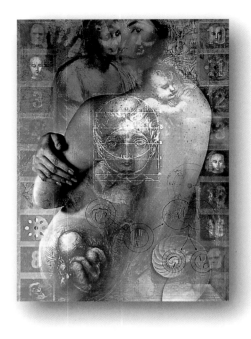

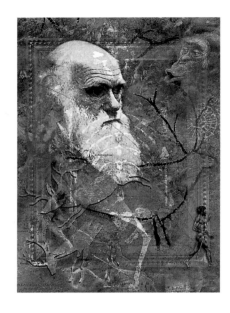

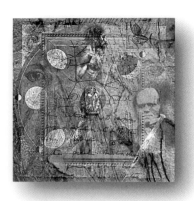

## DARWINIAN MEDICINE

*PHOTOGRAPHER*
**Scott Ferguson**

*DIGITAL CREATIVE*
**Scott Ferguson**

*ART DIRECTOR*
**Richard Boddy**

*CLIENT*
**Discover Magazine**

*SOFTWARE*
**Live Picture, Fractal Design's Painter, Adobe Illustrator, Adobe Photoshop**

*CATEGORY*
**Editorial**

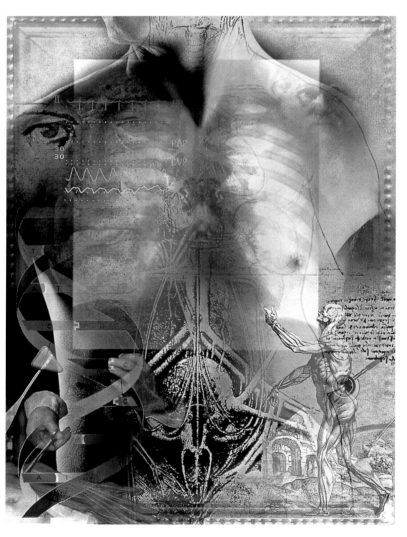

*editorial* EDITORIAL

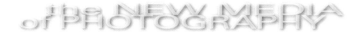
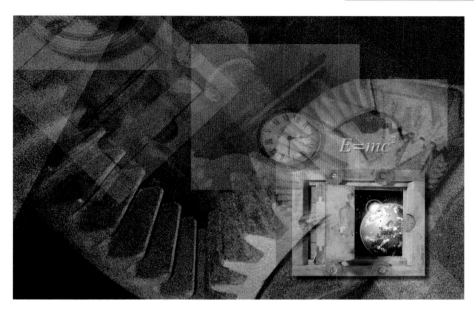

## HIGHER LEARNING EDUCATION

*PHOTOGRAPHER*
**Bill Milne**

*DIGITAL CREATIVE*
**Bill Milne**

*CLIENT*
**Sterling Publishing**

*SOFTWARE*
**Adobe Photoshop**

*CATEGORY*
**Book Cover**

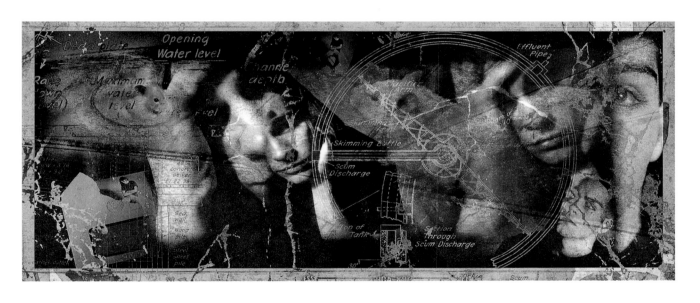

## SCHIZOPHRENIA

*PHOTOGRAPHER*
**Scott Ferguson**

*DIGITAL CREATIVE*
**Scott Ferguson**

*ART DIRECTOR*
**Richard Boddy**

*CLIENT*
**Discover Magazine**

*SOFTWARE*
**Live Picture, Fractal Design's
Painter, Adobe Illustrator,
Adobe Photoshop**

*CATEGORY*
**Editorial**

## THE FUTURE OF CHECKING

**PHOTOGRAPHER**
William Whitehurst

**DIGITAL CREATIVE**
William Whitehurst

**CLIENT**
ABA Banking Journal

**SOFTWARE**
Adobe Photoshop, Live Picture

**CATEGORY**
Editorial

## MULTIMEDIA COSTS

**PHOTOGRAPHER**
Joseph Kelter

**DIGITAL CREATIVE**
BadCat Design, Inc.

**CLIENT**
Upside Publishing

**SOFTWARE**
Specular Collage, Infini-D,
Adobe Photoshop

**CATEGORY**
Editorial

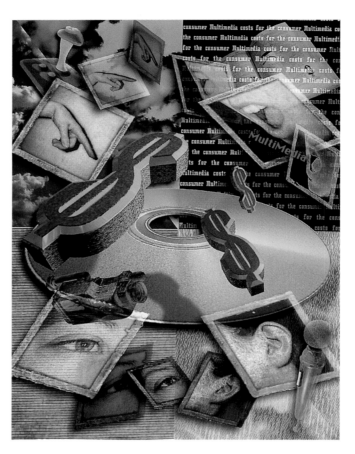

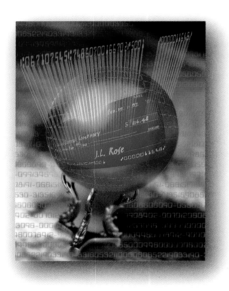

## SOFTWARE RIPS

**PHOTOGRAPHER**
Joseph Kelter

**DIGITAL CREATIVE**
BadCat Design, Inc.

**CLIENT**
Publish Magazine

**SOFTWARE**
Specular Collage, Infini-D,
Adobe Photoshop

**CATEGORY**
Editorial

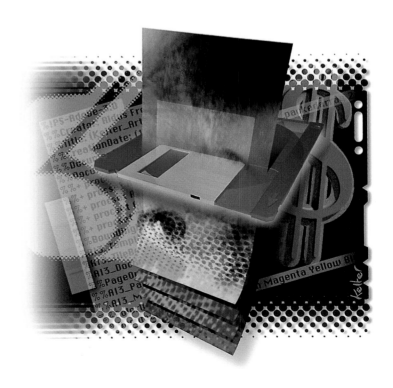

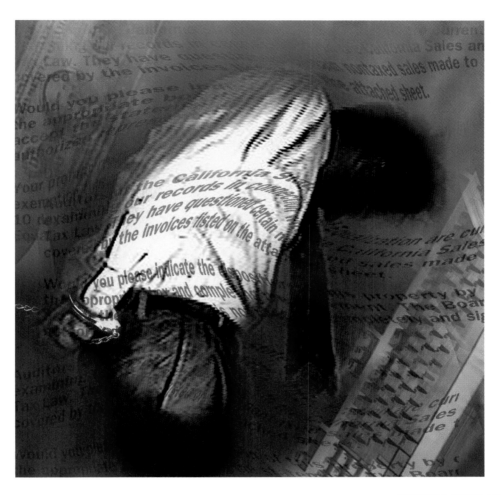

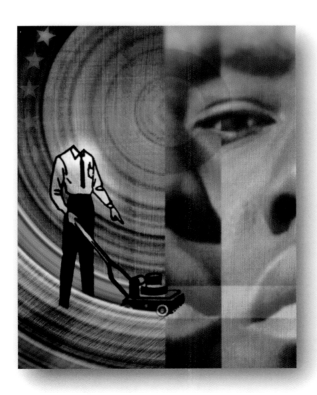

## DIGITAL TIME. BUSTED

*PHOTOGRAPHY & VIDEO*
Susan McMullen

*DIGITAL CREATIVE*
Lisa Webber

*CLIENT*
IBM

*SOFTWARE*
Adobe Photoshop

*CATEGORY*
Editorial

## POP AMERICAN LAWNS

*PHOTOGRAPHER*
Steve Mungay

*DIGITAL CREATIVE*
Paul Watson

*CLIENT*
Precision Craft

*SOFTWARE*
Adobe Photoshop

*CATEGORY*
E-Zine

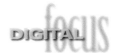

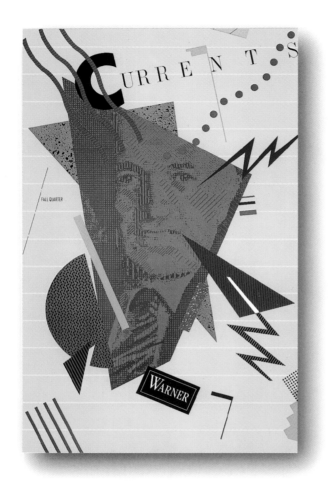

## CURRENT

**DIGITAL CREATIVE**
JRDG

**CLIENT**
Warner Communications

**SOFTWARE**
Mac Paint

**CATEGORY**
Quarterly Report Cover

## BUGS

**DIGITAL CREATIVE**
Eric Berendt

**CLIENT**
Compuserve Magazine

**SOFTWARE**
Adobe Photoshop,
Adobe Illustrator

**CATEGORY**
Editorial

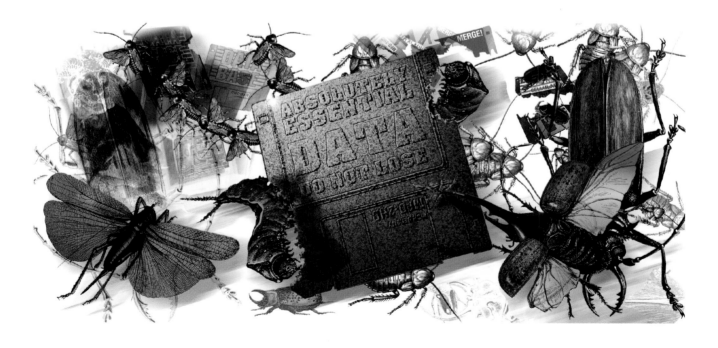

*editorial*

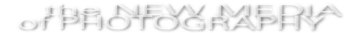

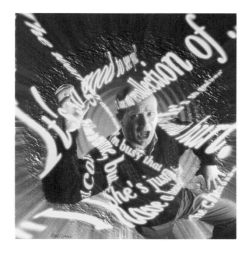

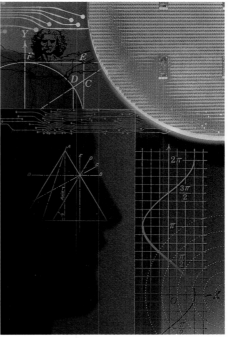

## IMAGINATION/KNOWLEDGE

**PHOTOGRAPHER**
Steven Hunt

**DIGITAL CREATIVE**
Steven Hunt

**CLIENT**
CRC Press

**SOFTWARE**
Adobe Photoshop

**CATEGORY**
Book Cover/Text

## WRAPPED UP IN LIES

**PHOTOGRAPHER**
Ed Lowe

**DIGITAL CREATIVE**
Philip Howe

**ART DIRECTOR**
Dianne Bartley

**CLIENT**
Kiwanis

**SOFTWARE**
Adobe Photoshop,
Fractal Design's Painter

**CATEGORY**
Editorial

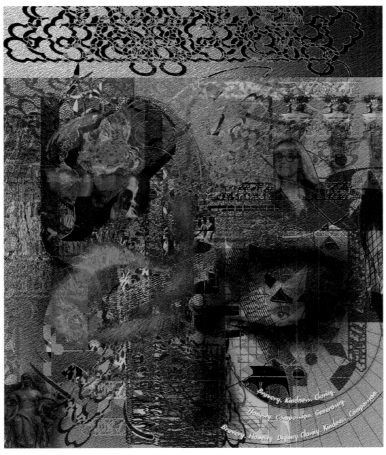

## FORGETTING

**PHOTOGRAPHER**
Stock

**DIGITAL CREATIVE**
Eric Berendt

**CLIENT**
Promotion

**SOFTWARE**
Adobe Photoshop,
Adobe Illustrator

**CATEGORY**
Editorial

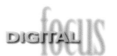

**PC I**

ILLUSTRATOR
**Jeff Brice**

ART DIRECTOR
**Joanne Hoffman**

CLIENT
**MacWorld Magazine**

SOFTWARE
**Adobe Photoshop**

CATEGORY
**Editorial**

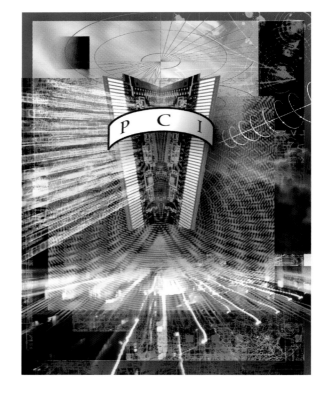

**WIDE WORLD WEBBERS**

PHOTOGRAPHY & VIDEO
**Lance Jackson**

DIGITAL CREATIVE
**Misiak**

CLIENT
**Compuserve Magazine**

SOFTWARE
**Adobe Photoshop**

CATEGORY
**Editorial**

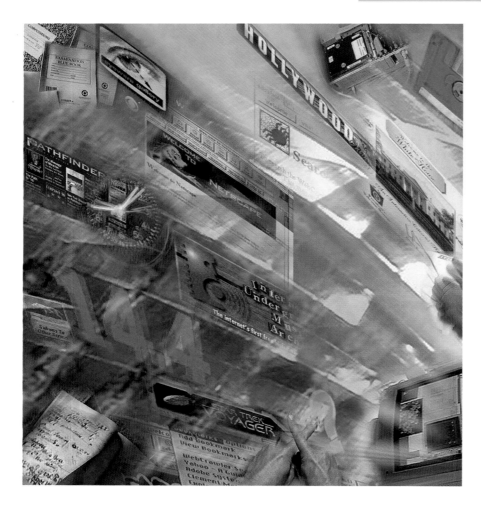

*editorial*

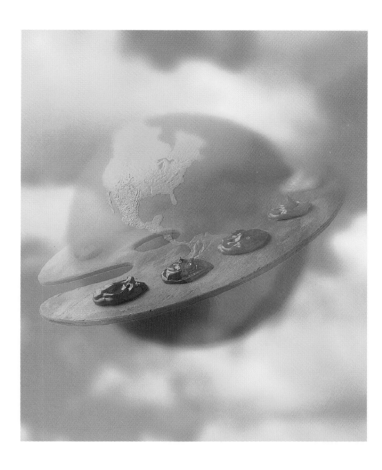

## GLOBE/PALETTE

*PHOTOGRAPHER*
Tom Collicott

*DIGITAL CREATIVE*
Tom Collicott

*CLIENT*
Moody Magazine

*SOFTWARE*
Adobe Photoshop

*CATEGORY*
Editorial

## HOURGLASS

*PHOTOGRAPHER*
Logan Seale

*DIGITAL CREATIVE*
Logan Seale

*CLIENT*
Logan Seale

*SOFTWARE*
Adobe Photoshop,
Photo Edges

*CATEGORY*
Editorial

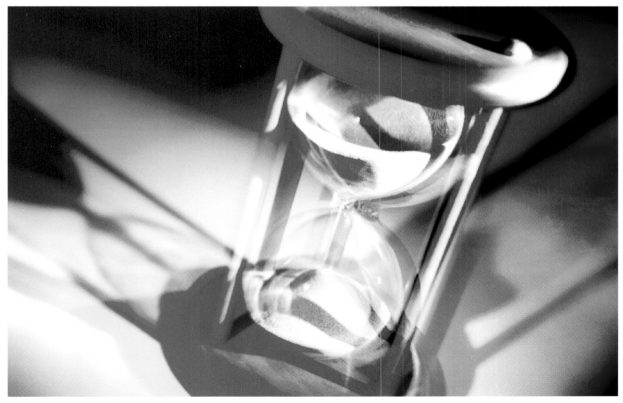

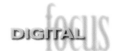

## AROMATHERAPHY BOOK

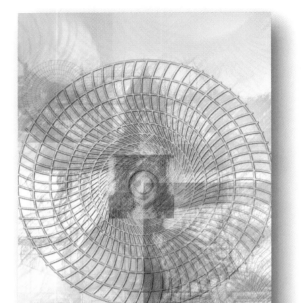

**PHOTOGRAPHER**
Bill Milne

**DIGITAL CREATIVE**
Bill Milne

**CLIENT**
Sterling Publishing

**SOFTWARE**
Adobe Photoshop, Adobe Illustrator

**CATEGORY**
Book Design

## SOCIAL TRIANGLES

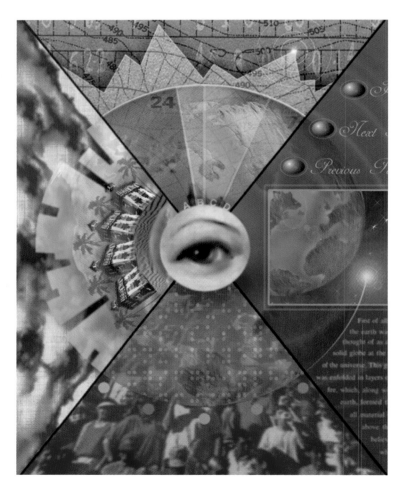

**PHOTOGRAPHER**
Paul Watson

**DIGITAL CREATIVE**
Paul Watson

**CLIENT**
Nelson Canada

**SOFTWARE**
Adobe Photoshop

**CATEGORY**
Book Cover

*editorial*

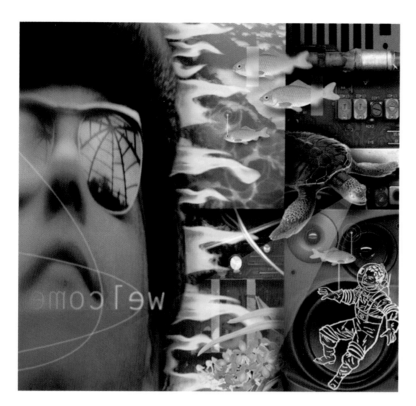

## ORBUS TERRARUM

**PHOTOGRAPHER**
Paul Watson

**DIGITAL CREATIVE**
Paul Watson

**CLIENT**
Request Magazine

**SOFTWARE**
Adobe Photoshop

**CATEGORY**
Music Magazine

## 3.0

**ILLUSTRATOR**
Jeff Brice

**ART DIRECTOR**
Joanne Hoffman

**CLIENT**
MacWorld Magazine

**SOFTWARE**
Adobe Photoshop

**CATEGORY**
Editorial

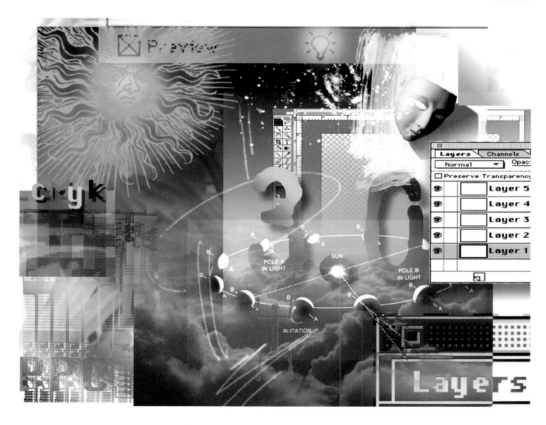

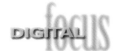

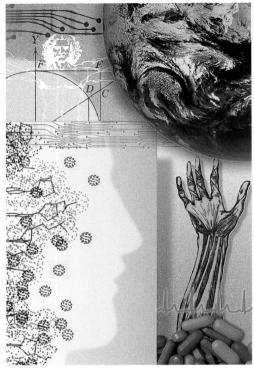

## COVER DESIGN

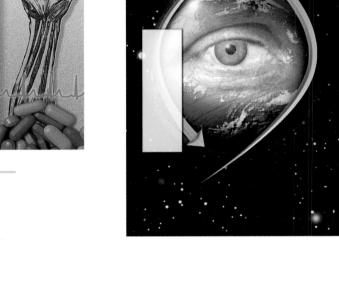

**PHOTOGRAPHER**
Bill Milne

**DIGITAL CREATIVE**
Bill Milne

**CLIENT**
Sterling Publishing

**SOFTWARE**
Adobe Photoshop,
Adobe Illustrator

**CATEGORY**
Hardcover Book Design

## MIRACLE MEDICINE

**PHOTOGRAPHER**
Steven Hunt

**DIGITAL CREATIVE**
Steven Hunt

**CLIENT**
PWS Publishing

**SOFTWARE**
Adobe Photoshop

**CATEGORY**
Editorial

## BLUE EYE

**PHOTOGRAPHER**
Logan Seale

**DIGITAL CREATIVE**
Logan Seale

**CLIENT**
Logan Seale

**SOFTWARE**
Adobe Photoshop

**CATEGORY**
Editorial

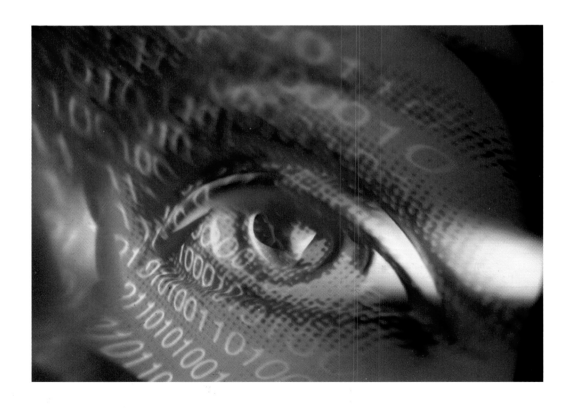

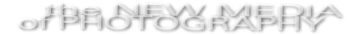

**BIOMETRICS**

*PHOTOGRAPHER*
William Whitehurst

*DIGITAL CREATIVE*
William Whitehurst

*CLIENT*
ABA Banking Journal

*SOFTWARE*
Adobe Photoshop, Live Picture

*CATEGORY*
Editorial

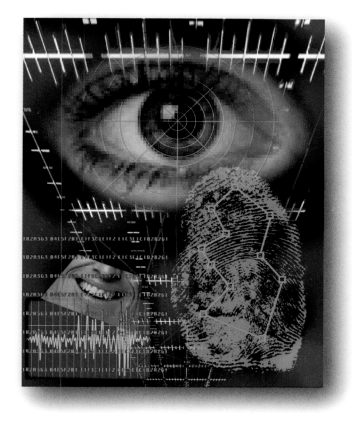

**SYNTHETIC SENTIENCE**

*DIGITAL CREATIVE*
Rob Magiera

*CLIENT*
Mondo 2000

*SOFTWARE*
Adobe Photoshop,
Alias Power Animator

*CATEGORY*
Editorial

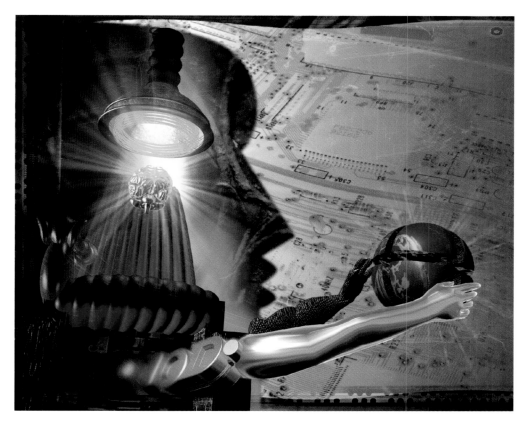

*editorial*

*promotional*

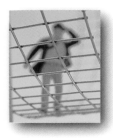

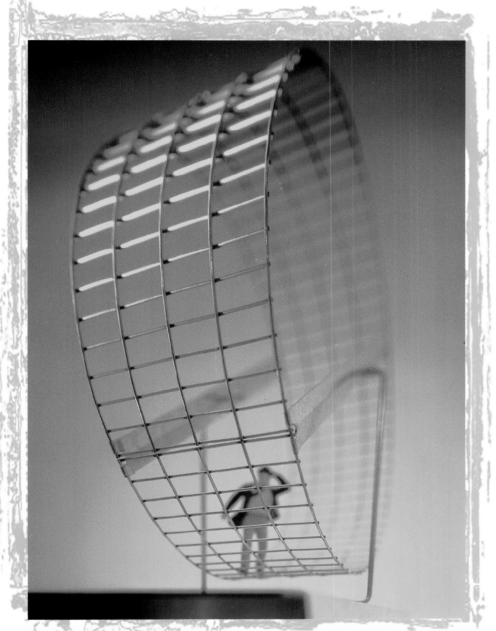

# STAN
## MUSILEK

The power of this image lies in its universally understood representation of human entrapment in an unending cycle of sameness. Originally designed as a self-promotion by Stan Musilek, depicting the unrealistic belief that everyone can achieve the American dream, this starkly provoking representation was later used with the image of a caged woman to advertise an anti-depressant.

The hamster wheel and the man were photographed against the same background and scanned into Adobe Photoshop. The integration of the elements was achieved using Live Picture, and the final composition was completed in Photoshop. Filters were then implemented to create the feeling of motion, enhanced lighting and a dramatically altered palette of color.

Musilek Photography has been producing compelling images for more than eighteen years. The advent of digital technology has expanded the range of their work and has given them the creative power to produce images that surpass time and space. Their contemporary vision has brought a wide range of large corporate clients including both Apple and Microsoft.

**RAT RACE**

*PHOTOGRAPHER*
**Stan Musilek**

*DIGITAL CREATIVE*
**Stan Musilek**

*CLIENT*
**Stan Musilek**

*SOFTWARE*
**Live Pictures**

*CATEGORY*
**Promotion**

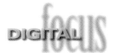

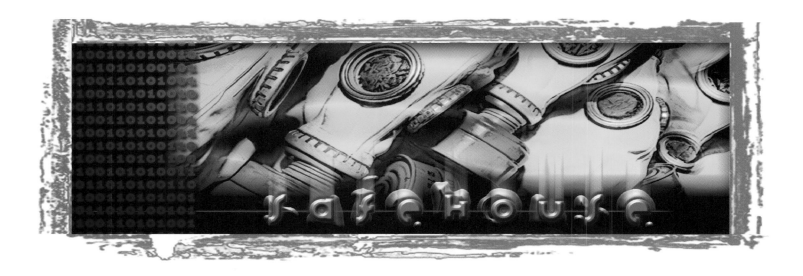

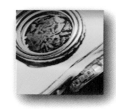

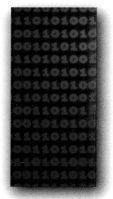

# MATTHEW PEACOCK

Anonymous Productions was given the challenge of developing a concise, visual identity for a newly formed recording company called Safehouse. By sampling the musical styles represented on the label, Matt Peacock transforms a futuristic and experimental sound into a striking graphic image that balances the brightly modern with the darkly industrial.

After the composition was developed on paper, it was scanned into Adobe Photoshop and used as a framework for the final piece. A stock image of a gas mask was imported into the program and integrated into the design. The text elements were produced in Adobe Illustrator and then saved as outlines. This step allowed for efficient manipulation and adjustments. The intense color palette and the final high resolution was completed in Adobe Photoshop.

Anonymous Productions is a fully digital design studio that specializes in cutting-edge visual applications. They work to create clearly focused imagery that reveals the client's true identity. With flexibility and insight, they find the perfect solutions for print, online and interactive multimedia projects.

**DIGITAL CREATIVE**
Matthew Peacock
Anonymous Productions

**CLIENT**
Safehouse Records

**SOFTWARE**
Adobe Photoshop,
Adobe Illustrator

**CATEGORY**
Business

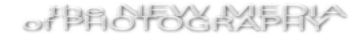

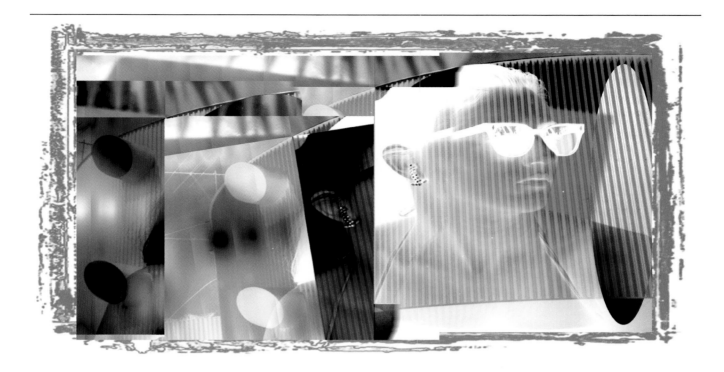

# RONALD DUNLAP

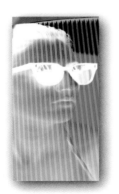

In this promotional spread by Ronald Dunlap, the repetition of pattern and soft colors captures a mood of warmth and mystery. Serving as an opening portrait in an actress' portfolio, the multiple image hints at her versatility in changing roles. The overlapping quality obscures detail and background information, and allows the viewer to conjecture thoughts about the woman behind the glasses. Her chameleon-like nature is further emphasized in the distinctly varied shades of her portrait.

Panoramic photographs were collaged several times, and adjusted in Adobe Photoshop using filters and color effects. Image reversing was applied to the original pictures. The elements were manipulated many times and a new coloration was added.

In this bizarre approach, Dunlap has taken the traditional headshot in a new direction. By concealing rather then revealing, power and excitement are established. Bringing a surreal exuberance and panoramic vision to his images, Dunlap demonstrates his own playful symbolism and shares the magical vision of his wideranging work.

### SHADE

*PHOTOGRAPHER*
**Ronald Dunlap**

*DIGITAL CREATIVE*
**Ronald Dunlap**

*CLIENT*
**Shaylee Dunn**

*SOFTWARE*
**Adobe Photoshop**

*CATEGORY*
**Business**

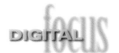

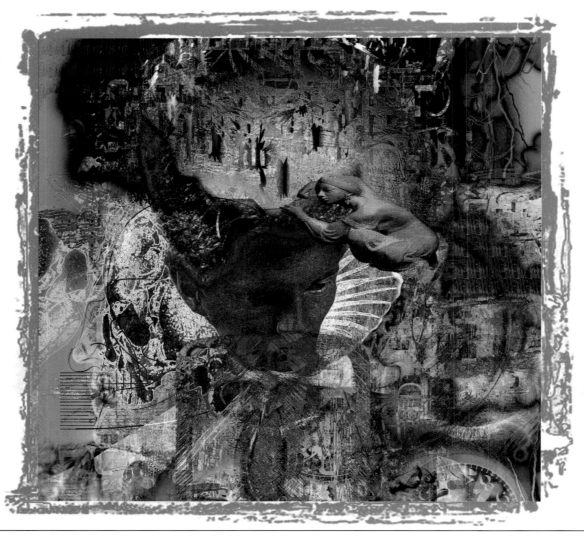

# ERIC BERENDT

Intricate and painterly, this image by Eric Berendt presents a delicate inner cosmology. Seemingly abstract, a long gaze allows faces to emerge and details seem to swim to the surface. It was created as a visual response to music by Philip Glass with inspirational lyrics by Susan Vega. He makes deliberate use of rhythmic elements as he interweaves a symbolic meaning of death and rebirth within the composition.

Besides his own paintings and drawings, Berendt collected public domain photographic and digital images and imported them into Adobe Photoshop. Using an approach akin to an abstract expressionist painter, he collaged, filtered and manipulated visual elements. He then recollaged and many additional filters were utilized. Final adjustments were implemented with color and texture.

The completed piece is a colorful and introspective exploration that transforms the aural into the visual. Music, nature and poetry are often the inspirational starting place for Berendt. With more than twelve years of experience, he integrates the traditional world of art with photography and digital technology. This provides a wealth of possibilities that he uses to create dynamic and soulful design solutions.

## LIGHTNING

**PHOTOGRAPHER**
Stock

**DIGITAL CREATIVE**
Eric Berendt

**CLIENT**
Promotion

**SOFTWARE**
Adobe Photoshop,
Adobe Illustrator,
Fractal Design
Painter

**CATEGORY**
Promotion

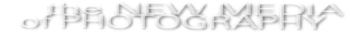

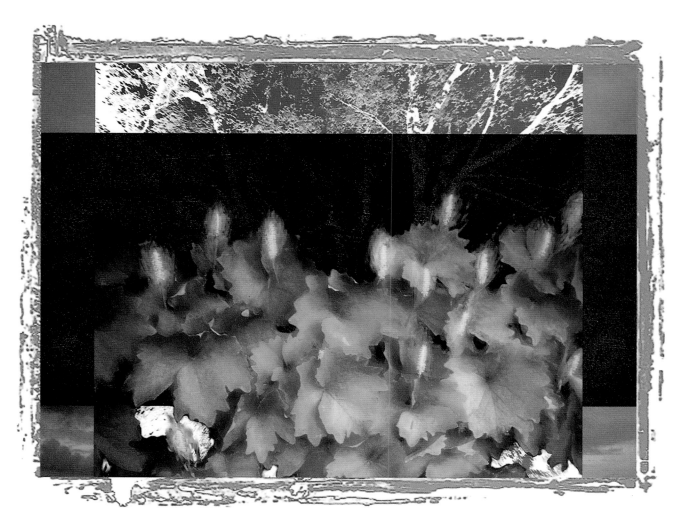

# KARIN SCHMINKE

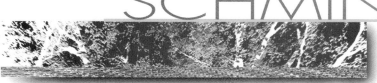

**EDGE OF THE FOREST**

*PHOTOGRAPHER*
**Karin Schminke**

*DIGITAL CREATIVE*
**Karin Schminke**

*CLIENT*
**Macromedia**

*SOFTWARE*
**Macromedia xRes**

*CATEGORY*
**Promotion**

Focusing on the simplest flora, Karin Schminke brings to life an enchanted Redwood forest. One of the largest graphics software companies, Macromedia, invited her to demonstrate the capabilities of a new software product called XRes. Schminke elected to create fantasy from the familiar. Through an exaggeration of organic elements, a fresh and magical landscape was formed.

Schminke's original photographs of trees and flowers were scanned and imported into Macromedia XRes. Filters were applied to the central image of the Vanilla Leaf flowers to enhance the violet edges of the green leaves and the vibrancy of the flower spikes. The tinted bands of surrounding color were fabricated within the program to restrain the lush flora, while the ghosted trees in the background anchor the piece both visually and conceptual.

Given the dual task of featuring photo-imaging and painting tools available in the software, Schminke's illustration offers a graceful yet sensitive solution. This engaging exploration fits into a larger body of work which focuses on the magic of the natural world.

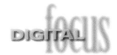

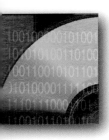

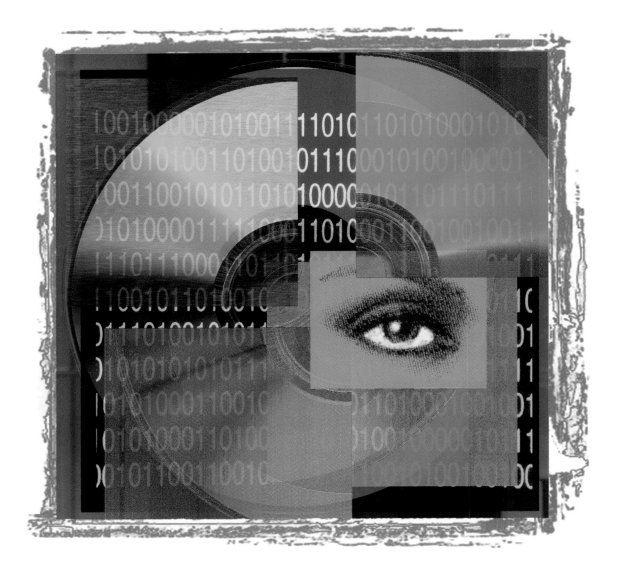

# LOGAN
## SEALE

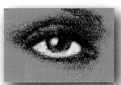

Logan Seale's commitment to the creative process allows him to transform the mundane into the marvelous. As with much of his work, this self-promotional piece emerged out of experimentation. He often starts with a simple question or curiosity. In this instance, Logan scanned a Gold Photo CD to see how the 3D object would be translated visually. This base image provided some surprising aspects that were interpreted and enhanced. The result is an abstraction of the literal — where meaning and design blend gracefully.

A scan of the CD was imported into Adobe Photoshop and then broken into layers. Working in Kais Convolver, fillers were applied to each layer. The image of the eye was culled from a CD of Seale's earlier photographic work and the final composition was arranged in Adobe Photoshop, using filters and a warm color palette. Through fragmentation and varying opacity, the ones and zeros of digital data become an active formal element; this suggests the connection between codes, language and visual communication. With more than ten years of experience, Logan's approach affords him the opportunity to bring a unique and effective point of view to each project.

**CD & EYE**

*DIGITAL CREATIVE*
**Logan Seale**

*CLIENT*
**Logan Seale**

*SOFTWARE*
**Adobe Photoshop,
Kais Convolver,**

*CATEGORY*
**Promotion**

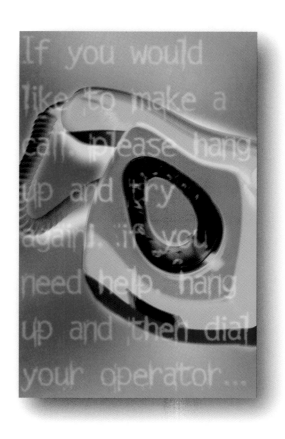

## PLEASE HANG UP

*PHOTOGRAPHER*
Caesar Lima

*DIGITAL CREATIVE*
Caesar Lima

*CLIENT*
Promotion

*SOFTWARE*
Adobe Photoshop,
Adobe Illustrator

*CATEGORY*
Promotion

## MAN TALK

*DIGITAL CREATIVE*
Rob Magiera

*CLIENT*
Self Promotion

*SOFTWARE*
Adobe Photoshop, Adobe
Illustrator

*CATEGORY*
Promotion

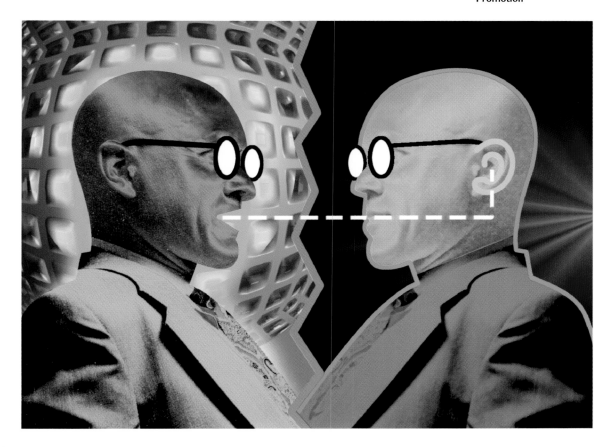

promotional

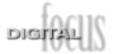

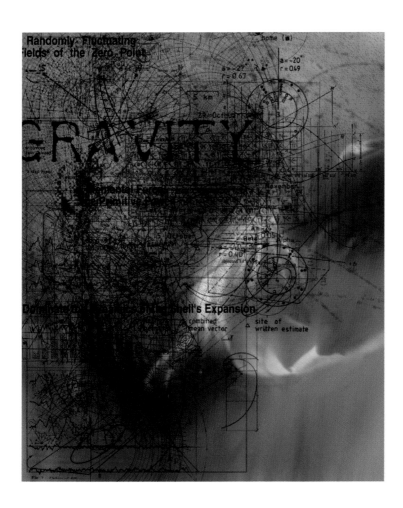

## GRAVITY

*ILLUSTRATOR*
**Jeff Brice**

*SOFTWARE*
**Adobe Photoshop**

*CATEGORY*
**Promotion**

## MAXIMUM RIGHTS MASK

*ILLUSTRATOR*
**Jeff Brice**

*CLIENT*
**Jeff Brice**

*SOFTWARE*
**Adobe Photoshop,
Specular Collage**

*CATEGORY*
**Promotion**

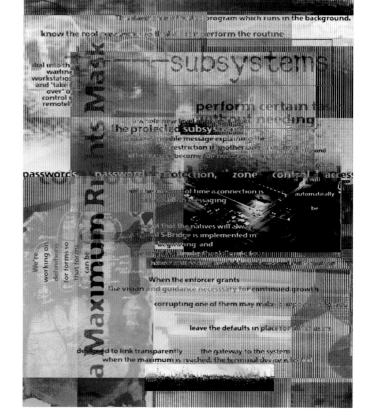

*promotional*

## QUEEN OF THE NILE

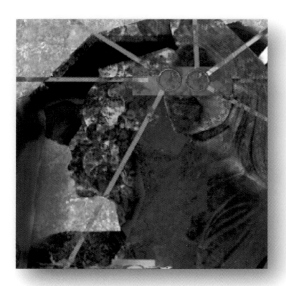

*PHOTOGRAPHER*
**Stock**

*DIGITAL CREATIVE*
**Eric Berendt**

*CLIENT*
**Promotion**

*SOFTWARE*
**Adobe Photoshop**

*CATEGORY*
**Promotion**

## UFO

*PHOTOGRAPHER*
**Jeff Brice**

*DIGITAL CREATIVE*
**Jeff Brice**

*CLIENT*
**Jeff Brice**

*SOFTWARE*
**Adobe Photoshop, Specular Collage**

*CATEGORY*
**Promotion**

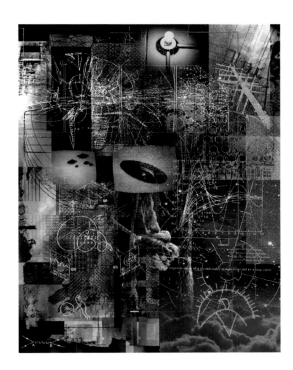

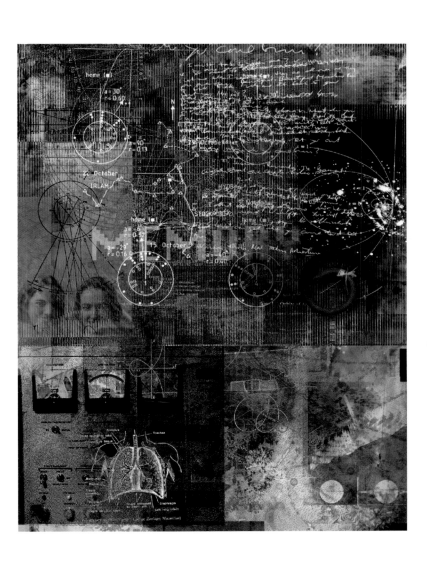

## MEMORY

*ILLUSTRATOR*
**Jeff Brice**

*SOFTWARE*
**Adobe Photoshop, Specular Collage**

*CATEGORY*
**Promotion**

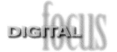

## KEYBOARD PUZZLE

*PHOTOGRAPHER*
Tom Collicott

*DIGITAL CREATIVE*
Tom Collicott

*CLIENT*
Tom Collicott Photography

*SOFTWARE*
Adobe Photoshop

*CATEGORY*
Promotion

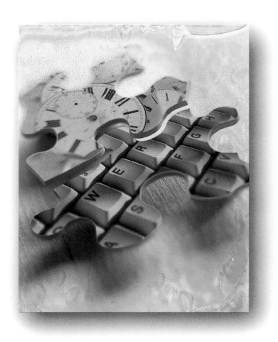

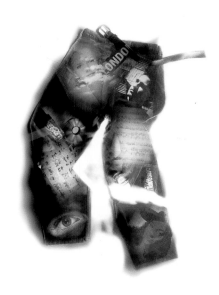

## PANTS

*PHOTOGRAPHER*
Ken Davies

*DIGITAL CREATIVE*
Ken Davies

*CLIENT*
Ken Davies

*SOFTWARE*
Adobe Photoshop

*CATEGORY*
Promotion

## GEARS

*PHOTOGRAPHER*
Tom Collicott

*DIGITAL CREATIVE*
Tom Collicott

*CLIENT*
Tom Collicott
Photography

*SOFTWARE*
Adobe Photoshop

*CATEGORY*
Promotion

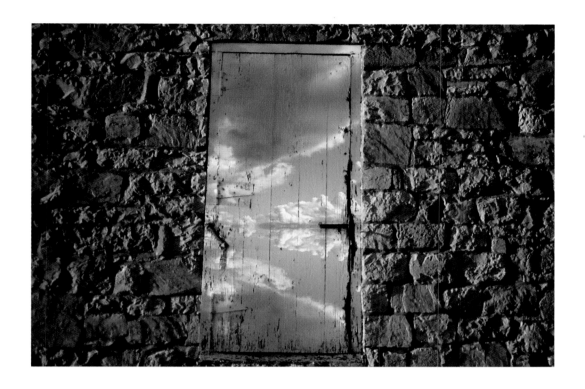

## CLOUDY DOOR

*PHOTOGRAPHER*
**Rick Dunn**

*DIGITAL CREATIVE*
**Rick Dunn**

*CLIENT*
**Rick Dunn**

*SOFTWARE*
**Adobe Photoshop**

*CATEGORY*
**Promotion**

## FLOATING LIPS

*PHOTOGRAPHERS*
**Sharon White/Bob Packert**

*DIGITAL CREATIVES*
**Sharon White/Bob Packert**

*CLIENT*
**White/Packert**

*SOFTWARE*
**Adobe Photoshop**

*CATEGORY*
**Promotion**

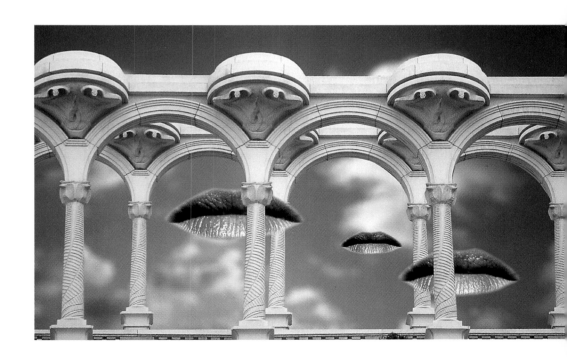

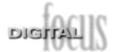

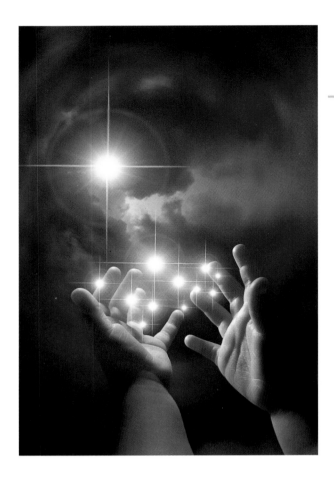

## OUR CHILDREN'S LEGACY

*PHOTOGRAPHER*
Steven Hunt

*DIGITAL CREATIVE*
Steven Hunt

*CLIENT*
Steven Hunt

*SOFTWARE*
Adobe Photoshop

*CATEGORY*
Promotion

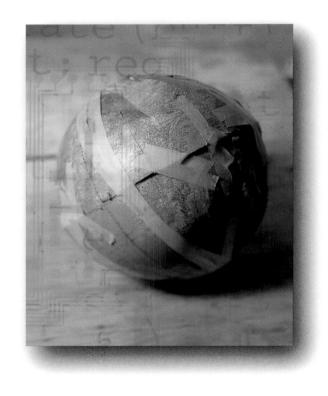

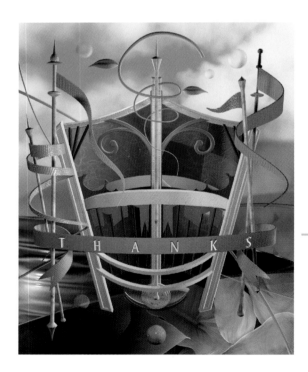

## THANKS

*PHOTOGRAPHER*
Stock, Henk Dawson

*DIGITAL CREATIVE*
Henk Dawson

*CLIENT*
Dawson 3D, Inc.

*SOFTWARE*
Form Z, Electric Image,
Adobe Photoshop

*CATEGORY*
Advertising

## TAPED GLOBE

*PHOTOGRAPHER*
Tom Collicott

*DIGITAL CREATIVE*
Tom Collicott

*CLIENT*
Tom Collicott Photography

*SOFTWARE*
Adobe Photoshop

*CATEGORY*
Promotion

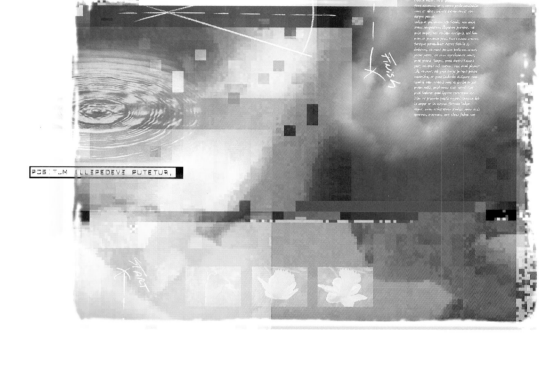

**SPEAK**

*PHOTOGRAPHER*
Video

*DIGITAL CREATIVE*
Dan Marcolina

*CLIENT*
Marcolina Design, Inc.

*SOFTWARE*
Video Capture,
Specular Collage

*CATEGORY*
Promotion

**RENAISSANCE**

*PHOTOGRAPHER*
Ronald Dunlap

*DIGITAL CREATIVE*
Ronald Dunlap

*CLIENT*
Doglight Studios

*SOFTWARE*
Adobe Photoshop

*CATEGORY*
Promotion

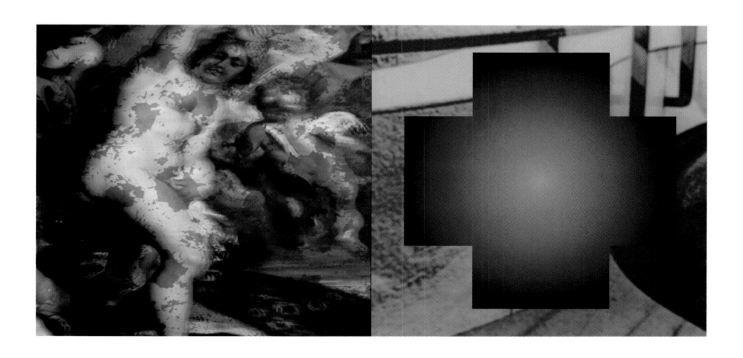

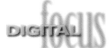

## SASSANIAN DREAM

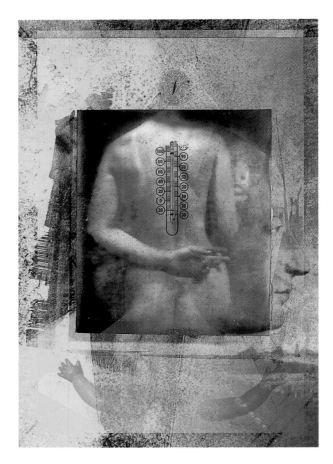

**PHOTOGRAPHER**
Scott Ferguson

**DIGITAL CREATIVE**
Scott Ferguson

**CLIENT**
Studio Promotion

**SOFTWARE**
Live Picture, Fractal
Design's Painter,
Adobe Illustrator,
Adobe Photoshop

**CATEGORY**
Promotion

## STRANGLE THE BETRAYER

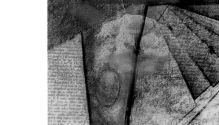

**PHOTOGRAPHER**
Scott Ferguson

**DIGITAL CREATIVE**
Scott Ferguson

**CLIENT**
Studio Promotion

**SOFTWARE**
Live Picture, Fractal Design's
Painter, Adobe Illustrator,
Adobe Photoshop

**CATEGORY**
Promotion

## LESSON LEARNED

**PHOTOGRAPHERS**
Joseph Kelter, Mia Park

**DIGITAL CREATIVE**
BadCat Design, Inc.

**CLIENT**
BadCat Design, Inc.

**SOFTWARE**
Specular Collage, Adobe
Photoshop, Fractal
Design's Painter

**CATEGORY**
Promotion

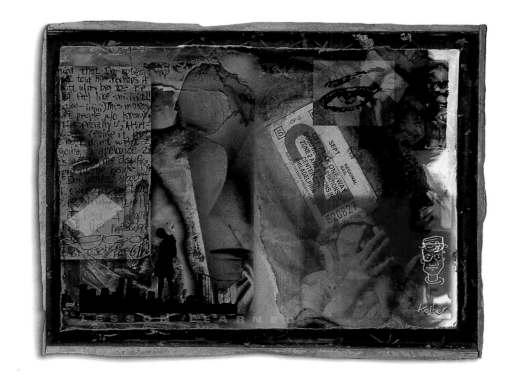

## ANGEL

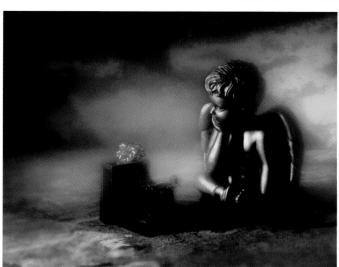

**PHOTOGRAPHER**
Michael Waine

**DIGITAL CREATIVE**
Michael Waine

**CLIENT**
Michael Waine Studio

**SOFTWARE**
Adobe Photoshop

**CATEGORY**
Promotion

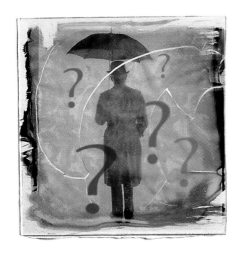

## QUESTIONS

**PHOTOGRAPHERS**
Sharon White/Bob Packert

**DIGITAL CREATIVES**
Sharon White/Bob Packert

**CLIENT**
White/Packert

**SOFTWARE**
Adobe Photoshop, Live Picture

**CATEGORY**
Promotion

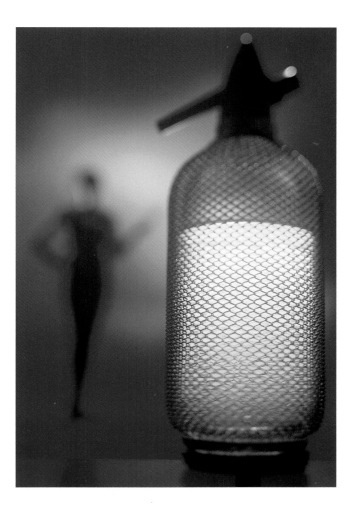

## SELTZER

**PHOTOGRAPHER**
Stan Musilek

**DIGITAL CREATIVE**
Stan Musilek

**CLIENT**
Stan Musilek

**SOFTWARE**
Live Pictures

**CATEGORY**
Promotion

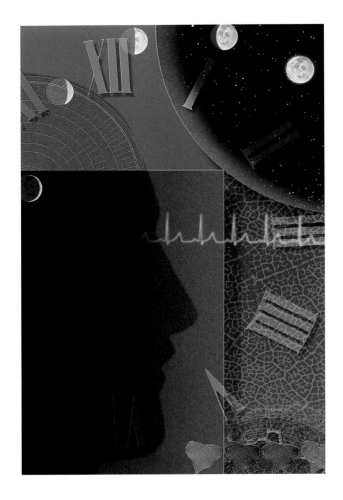

## RHYTHMS OF LIFE

PHOTOGRAPHER
Steven Hunt

DIGITAL CREATIVE
Steven Hunt

CLIENT
Steven Hunt

SOFTWARE
Adobe Photoshop

CATEGORY
Promotion

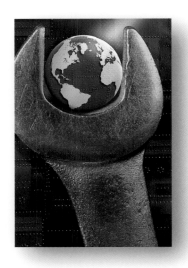

## TIME IS CHANGE, TRANSFORMATION, EVOLUTION

PHOTOGRAPHER
Steven Hunt

DIGITAL CREATIVE
Steven Hunt

CLIENT
Steven Hunt

SOFTWARE
Adobe Photoshop

CATEGORY
Promotion

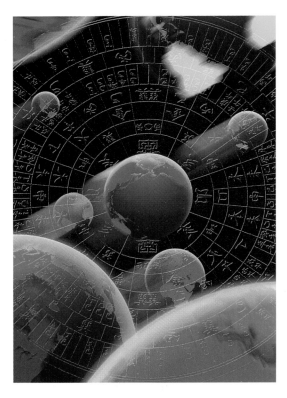

## WRENCH

PHOTOGRAPHER
Steven Hunt

DIGITAL CREATIVE
Steven Hunt

CLIENT
Stock Image

SOFTWARE
Adobe Photoshop

CATEGORY
Promotion

*promotional*

## DUALITY & DIVISION

**PHOTOGRAPHER**
Joseph Kelter, Various Stock Images

**DIGITAL CREATIVE**
BadCat Design, Inc.

**CLIENT**
Specular International

**SOFTWARE**
Specular Collage, Adobe Photoshop

**CATEGORY**
Promotion

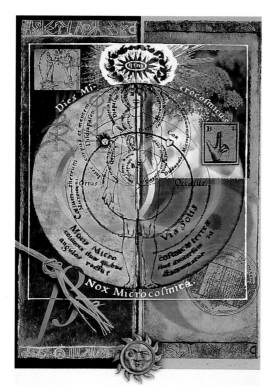

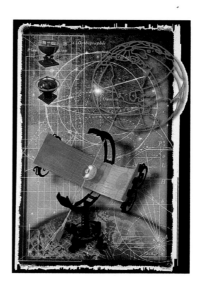

## NEW WORLDS

**PHOTOGRAPHER**
Joseph Kelter, Various Stock Images

**DIGITAL CREATIVE**
BadCat Design, Inc.

**CLIENT**
Ray Dream, Inc.

**SOFTWARE**
Ray Dream Designer, Adobe Photoshop

**CATEGORY**
Promotion

## TRANSFORMATIONS OF MAN

**PHOTOGRAPHER**
Steven Hunt

**DIGITAL CREATIVE**
Steven Hunt

**CLIENT**
Steven Hunt

**SOFTWARE**
Adobe Photoshop

**CATEGORY**
Promotion

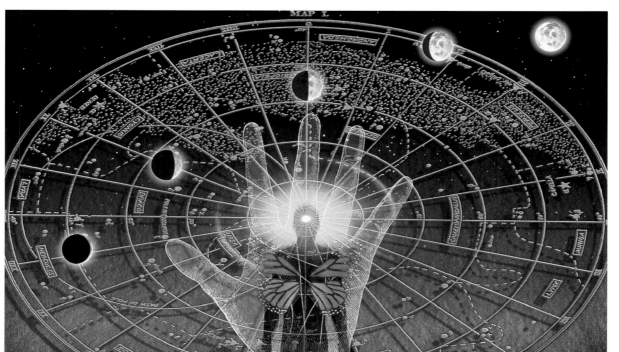

# EXPERIMENTAL

## experimental

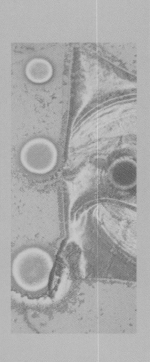

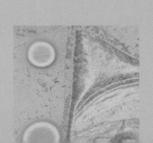

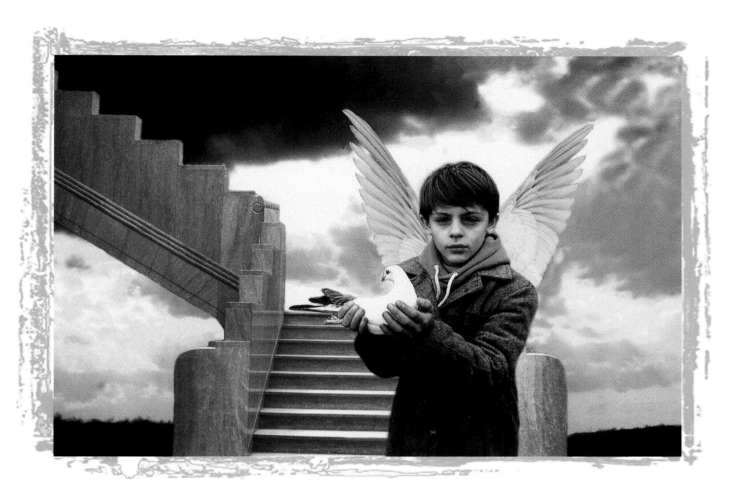

# DAVID CHALK

**BOY WITH WINGS**

*PHOTOGRAPHER*
**David Chalk**

*DIGITAL CREATIVE*
**David Chalk**

*CLIENT*
**ChalkMark Graphics**

*SOFTWARE*
**Barco Creator**

*CATEGORY*
**Experimental**

Throughout David Chalk's twenty-five year career, he has allowed his personal and commercial work to evolve simultaneously. This serenely symbolic image began with the discovery of one of his earliest commercial photographs featuring the boy holding a bird. The original photo was commissioned for a children's magazine article about homing pigeons. The mythical quality inspired him to fuse it with his contemporary images.

For this composite Chalk used his Silicon Graphics workstation and Barco Creator software, he started with a dramatic sky background shot in Soviet Central Asia. A section of a staircase from a Travel Holiday Magazine assignment was added to the composition. Chalk then used Creator's warping tool to create a pair of wings from a single image and fit them to the boy's body. The final output was an Iris print on Arches Watercolor paper further enhancing the magical atmosphere.

Working with a simple set of metaphoric signs, the image transforms the average into the sublime. The symbol of the dove and the repetition of the wings on the boy, suggest the sacred nature of the human spirit. This mystical image is the emergence of a new series on Urban Mythology to be produced over the next year. Recognized as a talented photographer, illustrator and animator, Chalk has an immense and diverse visual range which allows him to both emulate and subvert reality.

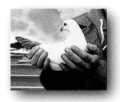

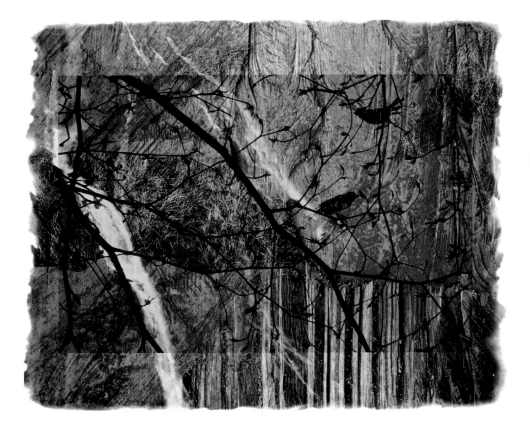

## TWO BIRDS

*PHOTOGRAPHER*
**Karin Schminke**

*DIGITAL CREATIVE*
**Karin Schminke**

*CLIENT*
**Karin Schminke**

*SOFTWARE*
**Fractal Design's
Painter, Adobe
Photoshop**

*CATEGORY*
**Experimental**

## SEPTEMBER

*PHOTOGRAPHER*
**Karin Schminke**

*DIGITAL CREATIVE*
**Karin Schminke**

*CLIENT*
**Karin Schminke**

*SOFTWARE*
**Fractal Design's Painter,
Adobe Photoshop**

*CATEGORY*
**Experimental**

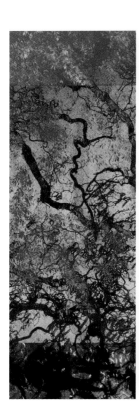
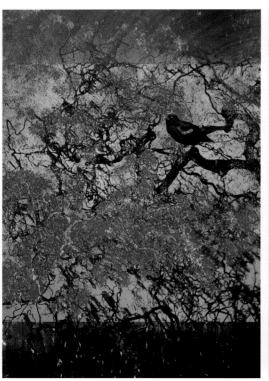
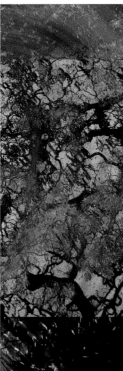

*experimental*

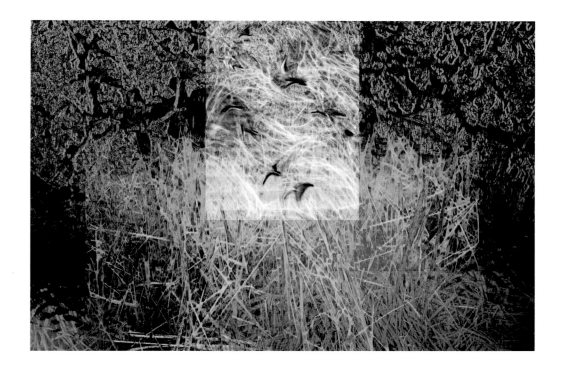

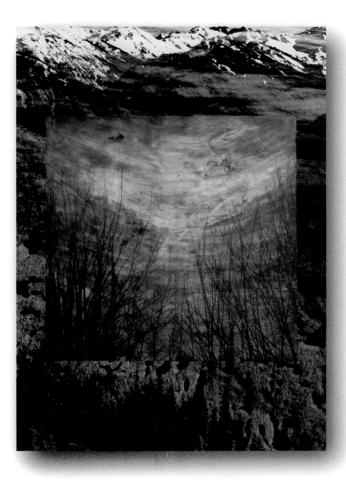

## PASSAGE

*PHOTOGRAPHER*
Karin Schminke

*DIGITAL CREATIVE*
Karin Schminke

*CLIENT*
Karin Schminke

*SOFTWARE*
Macromedia xRes,
Fractal Design's Painter,
Adobe Photoshop

*CATEGORY*
Experimental

## MOUNTAIN MEADOW

*PHOTOGRAPHER*
Karin Schminke

*DIGITAL CREATIVE*
Karin Schminke

*CLIENT*
Karin Schminke

*SOFTWARE*
Fractal Design's Painter,
Adobe Photoshop

*CATEGORY*
Experimental

*experimental*

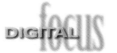

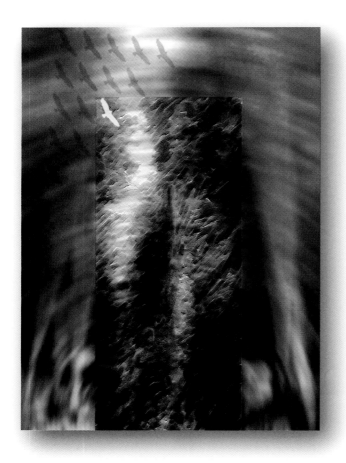

## NIGHT VISIONS

*PHOTOGRAPHER*
**Karin Schminke**

*DIGITAL CREATIVE*
**Karin Schminke**

*CLIENT*
**Karin Schminke**

*SOFTWARE*
**Fractal Design's
Painter, Adobe
Photoshop**

*CATEGORY*
**Experimental**

## ROOTS/WATER

*PHOTOGRAPHER*
**Karin Schminke**

*DIGITAL CREATIVE*
**Karin Schminke**

*CLIENT*
**Karin Schminke**

*SOFTWARE*
**Fractal Design's
Painter, Adobe
Photoshop**

*CATEGORY*
**Experimental**

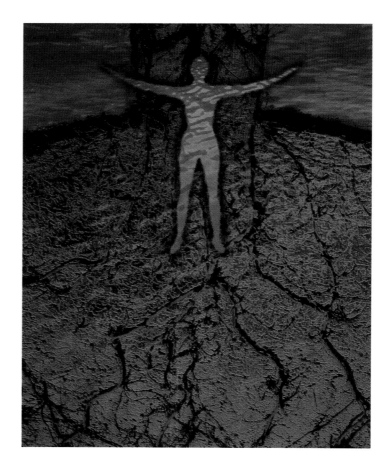

*experimental*

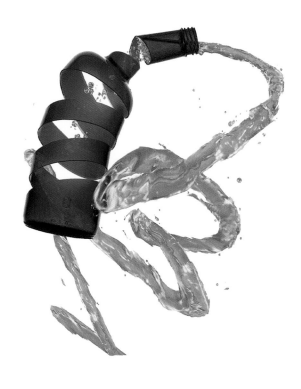

### RYE TWIST

*PHOTOGRAPHER*
**Barry Blackman**

*DIGITAL CREATIVE*
**Barry Blackman**

*CLIENT*
**Barry Blackman**

*SOFTWARE*
**Barco Creator**

*CATEGORY*
Experimental

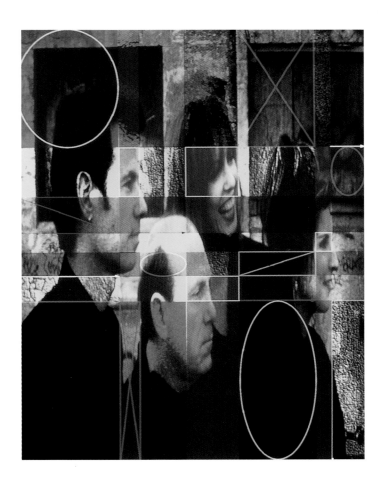

### GEOMETRIC PEOPLE

*PHOTOGRAPHER*
**Richard Duardo**

*DIGITAL CREATIVE*
**Tim Alt**

*CLIENT*
**Manhattan Transfer**

*SOFTWARE*
**Adobe Photoshop,
Macromedia Freehand**

*CATEGORY*
**Experimental**

*experimental*

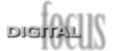

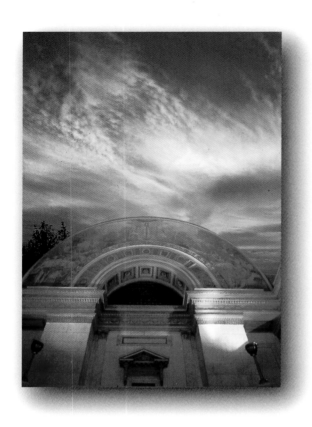

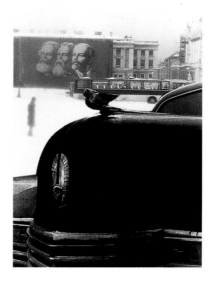

## EAST MEETS WEST

*PHOTOGRAPHER*
**David Chalk**

*DIGITAL CREATIVE*
**David Chalk**

*CLIENT*
**ChalkMark Graphics**

*SOFTWARE*
**Adobe Photoshop**

*CATEGORY*
**Experimental**

## ARCHWAY/SKY

*PHOTOGRAPHER*
**David Chalk**

*DIGITAL CREATIVE*
**David Chalk**

*CLIENT*
**ChalkMark Graphics**

*SOFTWARE*
**Adobe Photoshop**

*CATEGORY*
**Experimental**

## ARCHWAY/TRAIN

*PHOTOGRAPHER*
**David Chalk**

*DIGITAL CREATIVE*
**David Chalk**

*CLIENT*
**ChalkMark Graphics**

*SOFTWARE*
**Adobe Photoshop**

*CATEGORY*
**Experimental**

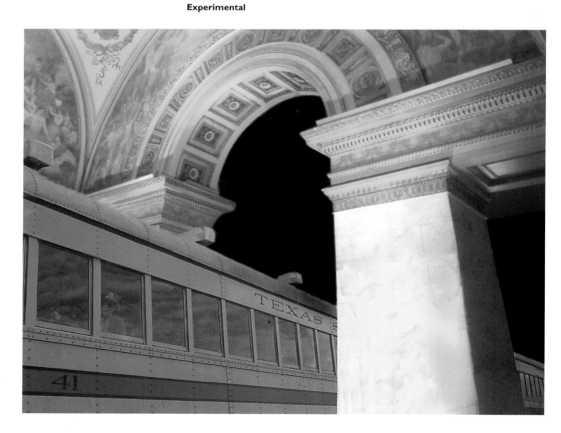

*experimental*

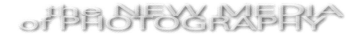

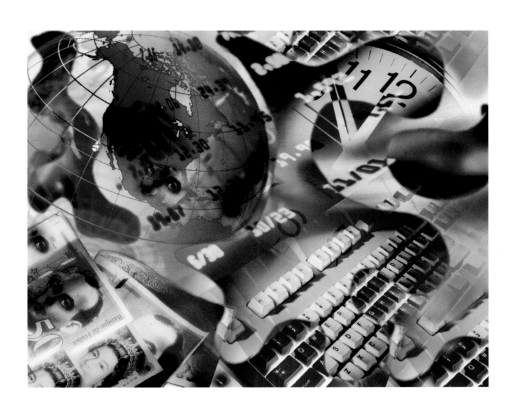

## POSNEG ADVENTURE

*PHOTOGRAPHER*
**Logan Seale**

*DIGITAL CREATIVE*
**Logan Seale**

*ART DIRECTOR*
**Brian Page/ONeil Communications**

*CLIENT*
**Digital Equipment Corp.**

*SOFTWARE*
**Adobe Photoshop**

*CATEGORY*
**Experimental**

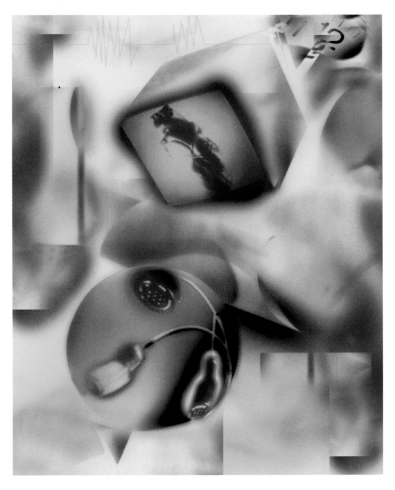

## MEDICAL EXPERIMENTS

*PHOTOGRAPHER*
**Logan Seale**

*DIGITAL CREATIVE*
**Logan Seale**

*CLIENT*
**Bard**

*SOFTWARE*
**Adobe Photoshop**

*CATEGORY*
**Experimental**

*experimental*

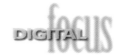

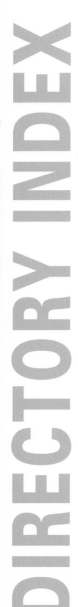

**Alt, Tim** • Digital Art
3166 E. Palmdale Blvd. / Suite 120 / Palmdale, CA 93550
**Phone:**805-265-8092 **Fax:**805-265-8095
63, 76, 77, 105, 107, 118, 171

**Berendt, Eric** • The Eric Berendt Studio
1989-A Santa Rita Road / #307 / Pleasanton, CA 94566
**Phone:**510-462-6809 **Fax:**510-462-6807
**Email:**eric@berendtstudio.com
**Website:**http://www.berendtstudio.com
114, 115, 118, 140, 141, 152, 157

**Blackman, Barry** • Cyber Kinematic Productions, Ltd.
Mendola Artist Reps / 450 Seventh St. / Ste 7A / Hoboken, NJ 07030
**Phone:**201-798-8990 **Email:**bstudio@hudsonet.com
**Website:**http://www.blackman-studio.com
32, 33, 78, 89, 111, 171

**Brice, Jeff**
Kolea Baker Artist Representative
2814 NW 22nd Street / Seattle, WA 98117
**Phone:**206-784-1136 **Fax:**206-784-1171 **Email:**jeffbrice@aol.com
44, 103, 121, 142, 145, 156, 157

**Burkey, J.W.** • Burkey Studios, inc.
1526 Edison Street / Dallas, TX 75207
**Phone:**1-888-216-6336 **Fax:**1-214-746-6338
**Email:**jwburkey@aol.com **Website:**http://www.jwburkey.com
13, 27, 78, 116

**Chalk, David** • ChalkMark Graphics
831 Clinton Street / #6 / Hoboken, NJ 07030
**Phone:**201-792-9658 **Email:**chalkman@concentric.net
114, 167, 172

**Collicott, Tom** • Tom Collicott Photography
Kolea Baker Artist Representatives
2814 NW 72nd Street / Seattle, WA 98117
**Phone:**206-784-1136 **Fax:**206-784-1171 **Email:**Tcollic@aol.com
37, 73, 102, 112, 113, 132, 143, 158, 160

**Davies, Ken**
11 Soho Street / Suite 201 / Toronto, M5T 1Z6 Canada
**Phone:**416-599-0240 **Fax:**416-599-5773
**Email:**kdavies@astral.magic.ca **Website:**kendavies.com
36, 44, 45, 55, 75, 79, 124, 130, 158

**Dawson, Henk** • Dawson 3D, Inc.
3519 170th Place NE / Bellevue WA 98008
**Phone:**425-882-3303 **Fax:**425-882-1005
**Email:**henkd@aol.com **Website:**http://www.henk.com/henk/
12, 96, 97, 129, 160

**Dunlap, Ronald & Honkawa, Tony**
Doglight Studios
600 Moulton Avenue / Suite 302 / Los Angeles, CA 90031
**Phone:**213-222-1928 **Fax:**213-222-8151
**Email:**doglight@aol or dogboys@doglight.com
**Website:**http://www.doglight.com
58, 59, 106, 151, 161

**Dunn, Rick** • Rick Dunn Studio
119 Paloma Avenue / Suite I / Venice, CA 90291
**Phone:**310-399-5263 **Fax:**310-581-5373
**Email:**rdunn@earthlink.com
**Website:**http://www.primenet.com/~rdunn
27, 62, 104, 108, 117, 119, 159

**Ferguson, Scott**
Ferguson & Katzman, Photography, Inc.
710 N. Tucker / Suite 512 / St. Louis, MO 63101
**Phone:**314-241-3811 **Fax:**314-241-3087 **Email:**fkphoto@aol.com
19, 88, 100, 112, 113, 120, 136, 137, 162

**Graham, Dale & Lemont, Vicky** • Ouch
57 Slade Street / Belmont MA 02178
**Phone:**617-489-8720 **Fax:**617-489-5730 **Email:**ouches@aol.com
86, 87, 90, 91, 92

**Howe, Philip** • Howe Computer Art
542 A 1st Avenue South / Seattle, WA 98104
**Phone:**206-682-3453/206-462-8790 **Fax:**206-623-2554
**Email:**dooder1@aol.com **Website:**http://www.catdaddygames
24, 81, 111, 128, 141

**Hunt, Steven** • PhotoDigital Illustration
2098 East 25 South / Layton, Utah 84040
**Phone:**801-544-4900
17, 24, 26, 141, 146, 160, 164, 165

**Ilic, Mirko** • Mirko Ilic Corporation
207 East 32nd Street / New York, NY 10016
**Phone:**212-481-9737 **Fax:**212-481-7088
126, 127, 129, 134, 135

**Jackson, Lance** • LSD AKA Lax Syntax Design
19 Los Amigos Court / Orinda, CA 94563-1605
**Phone:**510-253-3131 **Fax:**510-253-3191
**Email:**lsd@ccnet.com **Website:**http://www.ccnet.com~/sd
18, 19, 89, 99, 108, 109, 139, 142

**Kelter, Joseph** • BadCat Design, Inc.
3006 Aquetong Road / New Hope, PA 18938
**Phone:**215-794-7570 **Fax:**215-794-3823
**Email:**kelter@badcat.com **Website:**http://www.badcat.com/
15, 23, 138, 162, 165

**Koudis, Nick** • Nick Koudis Studio
30 W. 22nd Street / New York, NY 10010
**Phone:**212-206-0606 **Fax:**212-206-0345
**Email:**koudis@portfoliocentral.com
**Website:**http://www.portfoliocentral.com/koudis
9, 29, 74, 75, 110, Cover Image

**Lima, Caesar** • Caesar Photo Design, Inc.
21358 Nordhoff Street / #107 / Chatsworth, CA 91311
**Phone:**818-718-0878 **Fax:**818-718-8846
**Email:**caephoto@aol.com
**Website:**http://www.caesarphoto.com/design
34, 35, 36, 70, 74, 110, 155

**Magiera, Rob** • Noumena
8400 Kings Cove Drive / Salt Lake City, UT 84121
**Phone:**801-943-3650 **Fax:**801-944-9522
**Email:**bigpixel@xmission.com
**Website:**http://www.xmission.com/~bigpixel
11, 54, 73, 80, 81, 119, 120, 147, 155

**Marcolina, Dan** • Marcolina Design, Inc.
1100 E. Hector Street / Suite 400 / Conshohocken, PA 19428
**Phone:**610-940-0680 **Fax:**610-940-0638
**Email:**marcolina@aol.com **Website:**http://www.marcolina.com
45, 50, 52, 56, 57, 63, 83, 131, 161

**Milne, Bill** • Bill Milne Studio Representative: Lisa Cichocki
140 West 22nd Street / New York, NY 10011
**Phone:**212-255-0710 **Fax:**212-727-9575
**Website:**http://www.billmilne.com
14, 20, 49, 55, 59, 62, 131, 137, 144, 146

**Musilek, Stan** • Musilek Photography
Rep: Freda Scott, Inc. / 1224 Mariposa St./ San Francisco, CA 94107
**Phone:**415-621-5336 **Fax:**415-621-1508 **Email:**msk1224@aol.com
20, 47, 71, 79, 106, 149, 163

**Nelson, Geoffrey** • Geoffrey Nelson Photography
2636 Broadway / Redwood City, CA 94063
**Phone:**415-365-9563 **Fax:**415-365-1955
**Email:**tilt@sirius.com **Website:**http://www.imagineworks.com/tilt
43, 48, 49, 52, 53, 60, 61

**Packert, Bob & White, Sharon**
White/Packert Photography
Artist Representatives: Amy Frith/Beth Breslauer
9 East Street / Boston, MA 02111
**Phone:**617-423-0577 **Fax:**617-423-0578
**Email:**wpphoto@aol.com **Website:**http://www./sound/image.com
21, 71, 123, 159, 163

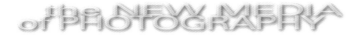
**Peacock, Matthew • Anonymous Productions**
403 Acorn Street / Lansdale, PA 19446
**Phone**:215-412-8210 **Fax**:215-393-8132
**Email**:design@anonymous1.com
**Website**:http://www.anonymous1.com
22, 66, 94, 95, 150

**Romero, Javier • Javier Romero Design Group**
24 East 23rd Street / New York, NY 10010
**Phone**:212-420-0656 **Fax**:212-420-1168
**Email**:javierr@jrdg.com **Website**:http://www.jrdg.com
22, 24, 93, 125, 140

**Schlowsky, Lois & Bob**
**Schlowsky Digital Photography & Computer Imagery Studios**
Representative: Lois Schlowsky
73 Old Road / Weston, MA 02193
**Phone**:617-899-5110 **Fax**:617-647-1608
**Email**:Bob@schlowsky.com
**Website**:http://www.schlowsky.com
41, 47, 60, 61, 64, 66, 67, 130

**Schminke, Karin • Woodland Associates**
Seattle, WA 98155
**Phone**:206-402-8606 **Email**:KSchminke@aol.com
153, 168, 169, 170

**Schneider, Carl • Carl Schneider Photography**
Artist Reps: West:Robert Lawrence 310-838-1704
Midwest/East:Lesley Zahara 800-670-2278
3770 Highland Ave. / Suite 203 / Manhattan Beach, CA 90266
**Phone**:310-545-9939 / 800-540-6008 **Fax**:310-545-6440
31, 35, 37, 38, 39

**Seale, Logan**
90 G Street / #4 / Boston, MA 02127
**Phone**:617-464-0400 **Fax**:617-464-3807
**Email**:logan@lsphoto.com **Website**:http://www.lsphoto.com
21, 110, 131, 143, 146, 154

**Wahlstrom, Richard**
**Richard Walstrom Photography, Inc.**
Artist Representative: Freda Scott
650 Alabama Street / Suite 302 / San Francisco, CA 94119
**Phone**:415-550-1400 **Fax**:415-282-9133
16, 26, 28, 77, 80

**Waine, Michael • Michael Waine Studio**
1923 East Franklin Street / Richmond, VA 23223
**Phone**:804-644-0164 **Fax**:804-644-0166
**Email**:mw@michaelwaine.com
**Website**:http://www.michaelwaine.com
10, 25, 27, 29, 163

**Watson, Paul • Paul Watson Illustration**
225 Sterling Rd. / Suite #9 / Toronto, Ontario M6R 2B2 Canada
**Phone**:416-535-2648 **Fax**:416-535-2648
**Email**:watson@passport.ca
65, 69, 72, 73, 139, 144, 145

**Whitehurst, William • Whitehurst Studio**
256 Fifth Avenue / New York, NY 10001
**Phone**:212-481-8481 **Fax**:212-481-8962
**Email**:williw@ix.netcom.com
46, 48, 50, 64, 65, 84, 85, 138, 147

**Yang, Eric**
213 LaFrance Avenue / #F / Alhambra, CA 91801
**Phone**:818-284-4727 **Fax**:818-282-5536
**Email**:etyang@aol.com **Website**:http://www.opticnerve.com
42, 51, 56, 132, 133

# DigitalFocus
## CALL FOR ENTRIES

DigitalFocus brings the diversity of imagination and provides a detailed examination of how digital and photographic creators have combined their talents to create a new photographic genre. The daring and ingenuity of imagemakers have transformed forever our understanding of the camera and the computer. Forty new visionaries will be selected to showcase their work.

## Categories Include:
Advertising, Business, Sports, Editorial, Surreal, People, Media, Promotional and Experimental.

## Preparation of Materials
Send slides, transparencies, photographic or laser prints. All work will be returned provided pre-paid packaging is provided.

## Deadline
Entries are accepted year round.
**Annual Deadline For Submissions November 15.**

## Please send to:
*Nick Greco / DigitalFocus Coordinator*
**Dimensional Illustrators, Inc.**
362 Second Street Pike/Suite 112
Southampton, Pennsylvania 18966  USA
215.953.1415 **Telephone**
215.953.1697 **Fax**
dimension@3DimIllus.com **Email**
http://www.3DimIllus.com **Website**

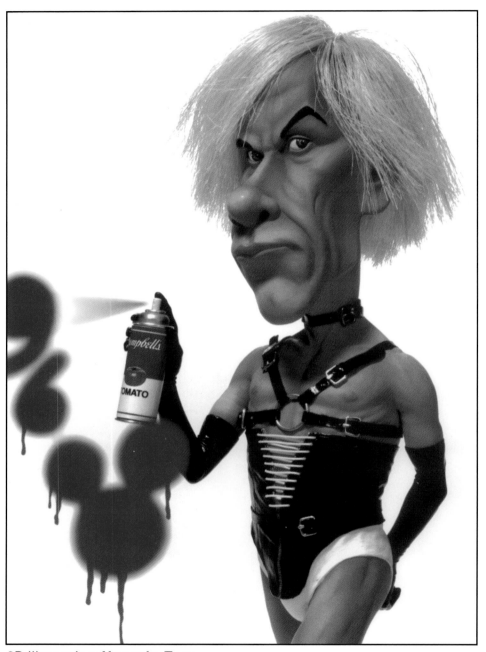